From the

Ash Heap

to a

Front Row Seat

Randy L. Williams

DEDICATION

I wrote this book for the caregivers of dying loved ones who cannot see a good future beyond the pending death before them. I wish to name Nina Kennedy Radford and Rachel Bradley Titus for being there with me during dark trials, and Ginger Schievers for her care of a dying husband and sister due to the same cancers that took two beloved mates of mine.

I also thank Ginger for being the catalyst that caused me to write what I swore repeatedly that I would never do. Although she is unaware of her role, Ginger's responses to the advice I shared during her trials, led me to think that maybe others could benefit.

FOREWORD

"Let us hold on to the confession of our hope without wavering, since he who promised is faithful. And let us watch out for one another to provoke love and good works,"
Hebrews 10:23-24 (CSB)

I met Randy when I came to First Baptist Riverview in August 1997. Nothing has changed from my first impression of him. He was this kind of silly, fun guy who loved God, family, and life. You would never know the intense military life he led.

It has been an amazing thing to watch Randy as he traversed this journey with God leading all the way.

What a great encouragement this book has been to me and many others I know as well. Randy shares his deepest hurts and emotions after dealing with the loss of not one but two wives to cancer. He opens up his heart as he takes you from the ash heap to the front row seat.

Randy's desire is that by sharing his journey you would be encouraged and comforted by his openness and honesty. Whether you're dealing with a loss of a loved one or just desire to draw closer to God, this is the book for you.

My prayer is that God will use this book in your life to encourage, uplift, and call you to watch out for one another and encourage love and good works toward those with whom you have influence.

Only God knows what the future holds for you on your journey through this life. You too might be called to some incredible opportunities.

Upon reading Randy's personal testimony, may your eyes be opened to a fresh new encounter with God.

Randall Hosea
Executive Pastor of First Baptist Riverview, Florida

CONTENTS

ACKNOWLEDGMENTS

I want to thank Pastor Randall and Kathy Hosea, Pastor Jeff and Sherri Butler, the Three Wise Men, and their wives, of the International Christian Fellowship of Kuwait, and sister-in-law Laura Stanley for reading the manuscript and providing sage advice.

I also thank Nina Radford, Joshua Williams and Laura Kvistad for the very fine editing. Joshua also has my deep appreciation for designing a book cover that captures the essential elements of the title, despite not matching the vision that birthed the title - pure genius.

It is to Evangelist Randy Bane of North Carolina that I credit learning evangelism by listening to numerous preaching services he delivered. He also invested time and great advice in me for several years after I was first saved, and he visited Kuwait to help the churches and conduct evangelism among the poor and downtrodden. While this manuscript does not take in those visits, I credit Randy for how I went about many of my efforts.

I deeply appreciate the direction, and editing and general advice to a rookie by authors Connie Bryson and Joseph Castagno. Thank you both for your books and confidence.

INTRODUCTION

In Acts 2:17 (NASB), the Apostle Peter quoted from the book of Joel 2:28-29: "And it shall be in the last days, God says, that I will pour forth My Spirit upon all mankind, and your sons and your daughters shall prophesy, and your young men shall see visions, and your old men shall dream dreams."

I will begin by saying that I am most uncomfortable writing about visions and whispered words of God. While I read of it in the Bible from years ago, and I hear preachers speak of it happening with them, it is not something with which I had personal familiarity. I had two reasons for even setting out on a project of recording words and visions from God. First, Pastor Dave Peacock in Kuwait insisted that I learn to write down any visions or words I receive from the Holy Spirit. He said we often misinterpret the significant part by focusing on what is meaningful to us, yet the real message is right there in the background details, but often overlooked.

The second reason is that in following what I am convinced is the leading by the Spirit of God I have become uncomfortable in my human logic with what I am doing. Yet I have a peace in my heart when I ask if I am to continue or change direction. I will admit that the Lord has had me handling my finances in a way that others might find illogical. But, there was always more than enough for me – maybe because I had no expensive hobbies any longer. After our first two military assignments had me away from our growing family a lot, I began saying that my first wife, Melissa, was my hobby. I spent the majority of my available time, money and energy doing things that included her, and usually the children.

Anyway, I will let this project unfold as best I can, and only withhold those items that the Spirit forbids me to record. Now, almost fifteen years after the first vision, I am probably suffering from forgetfulness of details and specific dates on some items. However, the overall gist and sequence I believe to be accurate. That project became the basis for this book that I never intended to publish in any form.

In this book, I try to describe my experiences with little or no attempt to fit them with Bible doctrine. While I have spent many months contemplating what occurred, I am still yet unwilling to say anything more than God seems unconcerned about the points of our various traditions. His grace will sometimes blow right through some narrative we have built up that prevents us from giving a second chance to a damaged person that the Holy Spirit has marked for His use in doing our Lord's will. I say this because the Holy Spirit directed me to do some things not in keeping with the traditions of my denomination on occasions. Also, I was often caught by surprise and then opted to follow my orders as best I was able to understand them at the time, rather than miss the opportunity while wrestling with such a matter less valuable than a soul. Time after time, His direction led me to see great good done in His Name. Yet, because of my own imperfections, I would pray to be faithful in my intentions as well as in how I did the things He asked of me.

I recently completed reading the Babylonian Talmud and saw how the majority of references to the Prophetess Deborah were uncomplimentary, despite it being God that gave her the positions of Judge of Israel and seer. As her guidance of Barak led to a great victory, I cannot help but wonder if sometimes the most highly-regarded religious scholars misjudge the individual that God uses for a single purpose because it does not fit their doctrinal or traditional view. Consider that maybe God did not get that specific memo from human scholars on how He should be doing His business.

When the Apostle Paul said, "We have no other tradition" (I Corinthians 11:16), he was certainly correct as far as his Pharisaical training was concerned, but the new faith, called Christianity, was figuring out its way of doing things that would later be called tradition. When I read his rhetorical question in verse 13, my response was not at

3

all in line with Paul's expectation – to see a woman pray with uncovered head is a pleasing sight rather than an affront.

I am also aware that some eminent bible scholars of our day have said that God no longer speaks audibly to man, so I fully expect criticism. I am beyond convinced that the Holy Spirit communicates with the children of God in many ways, to include dreams and spoken words. But honestly, dear reader, there have been times I had to ask myself, "Why would the Holy Spirit pick a flawed human like myself for this work?" Or just as often ask, "Am I losing my mind?"

My primary aim in writing this book is twofold: To encourage those who find themselves being guided by our Heavenly Father in ways that defy logic; and to pass on practical advice to caregivers and those who have lost loved ones so they maintain hope and understand that their lives should not end with the death of others. While I have been encouraged to write my story, it seems so personal as to only be of value to my family.

Although I spent over twenty-five years in the U.S. Army, this book is not about military service. Yet, I see God has a certain sense of humor in taking me from that life into new chapters requiring greater empathy than I had ever possessed. Since those days of military service, I have waded into a group of Sri Lankan women caught up in human trafficking while only seeing the mission and missed the incongruity of being in a place where my almost purely masculine experiences counted very little.

My religious instruction from an early age occurred in a Missionary Baptist Church as my mother insured my brothers and I attended both Sunday services and the Wednesday evening service. Now that I am assisting my parents run their farm, I am again accompanying them to another church of the same affiliation. During a recent Sunday School service in August of 2018, I read something disturbing from literature produced by the American Baptist Association. In this quarterly, it stated, *"A dream is just a dream. There is no hidden meaning to our dreams, and God is not making an attempt to communicate with us through them. There is a channel of revelation from God, the Word of God. If you want to know more about the hidden things of eternity and get a message from God, read your Bible."* Not only are there no Scriptures to back that up, I think I learned the source of my ignorance to the various workings of the Holy Spirit.

You will see as this story unfolds, that I was caught completely off guard when God the Holy Spirit did communicate with me by means other than the Bible. For the record, I have not included every word, dream, vision or experience, but only those that best describe my journey and those I felt I had permission to share.

In closing, I recently sent an email to a pastor and his wife who were a part of this story in the early years, and told them that if I publish this book, I will likely disqualify myself from ever serving in any mainstream denomination as a pastor. That may very well prove true. Oddly, this couple responded that if this book disqualifies me in that manner, then there must be something worth reading in its pages. It is my prayer that they are correct and that you, my dear reader, find nuggets along the way. God bless you as you work out your faith!

Chapter 1. Loss of My Mate - Beginning of Visions

"Precious in the sight of the Lord
is the death of His saints."
Psalms 116:15 (ESV)

The Moment of Realization
(Origin of the Book Title)

I find in Scripture that we are saved for a purpose, created for good works, bought with a price. My life is not mine to throw away regardless how deep my grief, so I went looking for a reason to keep going with a fresh set of eyes.

It was late August, 2005. The mixture of paint and gloss, used for the rag-on/rag-off technique of application, had finally dried. I was now able to place the remaining treasures from our time in the Middle East and Southern Asia in the proper places. I called out, "Ta-da! It is finished!" Now the home I'd promised Melissa years ago for her faithful service as an Army wife was complete. I turned to see a broad smile and a bright light in her green eyes. These features stood out from the scarecrow-like body so ravaged by her two-year battle with a recurrence of colon cancer. She had chosen the place, designed the house, and picked out the colors for the home where we'd intended to grow old together. This was the dreamed-for place where we looked to spoil a crop of grandchildren from our three sons.

I had worked like a madman since May, that is, whenever I wasn't performing my duties as an Army officer with U.S. Central Command, to accomplish this feat. Now that it was done, I realized that I had no other important goal to set my hand to do! She had mere weeks left to live, and as I looked to the future in that moment, suddenly an inky-black velvet curtain dropped across our path. I could only see a scatter of ashes before that veil. This labor of love into which I had poured much time and great expense would become valueless without Melissa.

From these ashes, a new life and set of goals would arise in the next chapter of my existence. However, those goals and any accomplishments would not be mine as God issued this old soldier new marching orders. I would just be going where I was told and taking a front row seat to watch Him accomplish His will. I could make no claim on those actions, just revel in the moment that He allowed me to be a witness to each of those events.

Then one morning during my devotional, I read in Deuteronomy 10:21, "He is your praise, He is your God, who performed those great and awesome wonders you saw with your own eyes." Immediately, I recalled thinking about the past twelve years and having that front row seat to what God did as I stepped out in faith. I'm reminded never to take credit, and so I strive to maintain that view each time I write or edit a section of this personal journey.

Background

Visions were not something common with me. In April of 1985, I believe Jesus Christ confronted me in a vision with my pretending to be a Christian and offered salvation if I would give my life to Him. I did give my life to Him as Savior and Lord, and have never regretted accepting that offer. I didn't have another vision until 2003, but I had learned to read Scripture and listen to Christian leaders and friends with an eye for illuminated passages. Other times, I would feel a catch in my spirit that there was something specific for me in what I had heard or read, or about a situation in which I found myself. In those cases, I needed to sit up and consider what it was that needed my attention or action.

I will say Melissa Ann (Simpson) Williams was my beloved on this earth. Just dumb kids it seemed, but we grew so close through the years.

Initially, I had been difficult while trying to learn to be a man, an Army Officer, and a husband. I felt as though I was barely succeeding on any of those points. Also, her parents' divorce four years later impacted us up to our eighth year of marriage. My beloved was special. She was my dearest friend and advisor whom I had been at a loss without until the Holy Spirit stepped in larger than life - and later brought me a second helpmeet, Sharon.

I will mention below how Melissa felt she had left no impact on this world, but I think it will be clear that she impacted many people, directly and indirectly.

Melissa Ann Simpson moments before our wedding, December 5, 1981 – Still my favorite photo.

After marriage on December 5, 1981, we had a difficult and impoverished time in Germany – but the distance from family support kept us close and the poverty made us work together. We were both raised in church, but did not know Jesus Christ as our Lord. When we returned to the U.S. for me to attend a military school in Georgia, Jesus saved me through the work of a dedicated Sunday School teacher named Jetty Morris, and the aforementioned vision of 1985. A few months afterward, Jetty was forbidden to teach any longer by the pastor for reasons unknown to me. Six months later, this pastor left the ministry because of an affair with a choir member. This was a confusing time for a baby Christian like me. Jetty and her husband seemed to take it all in stride, but then I lost contact with them. I certainly hoped they returned to that ministry that they were so gifted to do.

During the next few years, I learned to hold daily quiet times and felt that the Lord gave me a ministry of sorts by supporting pastors and teaching Sunday School since no more mature believer would step up. I grew much, but was still just a youth in Christianity. Good thing my faith had grown, because only two years later, I was tested in my faith by a commander who demanded I go along with unethical treatment of a sergeant. Melissa helped me stay the course as we faced the impending loss of my military career. Then suddenly, this commander was fired due to circumstances having nothing to do with me. We weathered that storm and came out stronger as a couple. In addition, I had developed a very solid reputation in the unit and with the new commander.

Melissa was a perfect mate for me and became my hero, as I was her hero. I knew of no man who could suffer as quietly as she did through the hated disease of cancer. She tried her best to make things as easy on the boys and me as she could. In the spring of 2005, sadly, she said, "It seems so unfair. You have become the husband I always dreamed of, and now I cannot be the wife you need." What higher compliment could any man possibly ask for than to know he had become the husband his wife always dreamed to have. I was speechless for a bit as my heart hurt for us both.

I grew up in a patriarchal clan, had only brothers and raised sons only, plus worked for many years in the Army infantry and Ranger units that were all male. When my former military guys in Kuwait volunteered to help me support many women left imprisoned as victims of human trafficking, I found an instance where I looked to the heavens and told God that he had terrific sense of humor. You see, these men loaded up the sleeping mattresses, toiletries, powdered milk and feminine hygiene products so that my SUV had all of the feminine hygiene items stacked to the ceiling in the front and back passenger seats so all passersby would not miss them. I wondered what my old Ranger sergeants would think of me if they saw this! Apparently, God knew just what I needed by breaking my heart so deeply and then having me come face-to-face with

9

350 women sharing two toilets, sleeping on concrete floors, and using a washroom with a busted pipe that caused the need for four types of foot fungus medication. He knew I would spring to action of some kind.... and I will tell you now that I know I can be a blunt instrument at times.

Beginning of Bad Times

The bad part began subtly while we were stationed in Jordan from 1993-1994. Melissa had a bleeding problem and went multiple times to doctors at one of Jordan's finest hospitals. They just kept testing for amoebas and parasites. She mentioned that these British-trained Arab doctors had no regard for the comments and feelings of women. I had attended one of the visits with her, but they still came up with nothing. She was worried but hid much of it from me. I had no such understanding of how attuned she was with the inner workings of her body.

We returned to the U.S. and a doctor at a small county hospital in upstate New York found the cause - an intestinal polyp. After the first visit, he immediately scheduled a procedure to remove and biopsy it. While she was gearing up for surgery, I was deeply involved in preparations for the invasion of Haiti. I had determined when my unit went to Haiti as part of Operation RESTORE DEMOCRACY, that if her surgery was serious, I would return to be with Melissa.

After twelve days aboard the USS *Eisenhower*, we air landed the invasion force by helicopter at various points around the country. I ended up at the Port-au-Prince airport. It was a Spartan environment to be sure. My initial focus was on getting water and food to the entire force around the capital, which included units beyond my brigade. Members responsible for resupply within these other units were directed to me to request support. The initial invasion plans had changed drastically in the past two days as the invasion became an Operation Other Than War. My brigade was now the main effort, so many non-Army units were looking for the right logistics center to plug into. Similarly, I was reporting to a Corp level asset (way above my normal duties) to draw rations as I became responsible for logistics for an estimated 6,500-man force in and around Port-Au-Prince on Day One. This continued until normal support chains could be re-established five days later.

The Mysterious Colonel Turner

On that first day in Haiti, God clearly gave me a conundrum. We had troops spread around a large area, and our commanding general suddenly ordered no vehicle convoys through the night due to fears of a backlash by possible Raul Cedras' supporters. All of our rotary wing assets were out at sea on the USS *Eisenhower* having mandatory crew rest. My brigade had one company of men out at the Haitian-American Sugar Company to secure it. That unit's battalion commander found me and made a personal plea to solve his dilemma. He told me that this company had run out of drinking water and had inserted its last bags of IV fluids in their four heat casualties. I knew we had no way of resupply with organic assets until morning. Out of ideas, I wandered out of the airport where our temporary headquarters was located and onto the dark runway. There, in a loud voice, I cried out to God for His help. Suddenly, and to my shock, an Army Colonel named Turner (by his uniform) walked out of that darkness and asked, "What's the problem, Major?" After I recovered from my shock, I described the situation and he asked me if I had a radio. I took him over to my Humvee and showed him my communications gear. He said he was from the 7th Transportation and had barges at the harbor that could deliver fresh water by hoses to the men if they could take their containers out onto the pier of the Haitian-American Sugar factory.

Colonel Turner made the arrangements with the barge unit in the harbor. I thanked him, and then made my calls down to the infantry unit and battalion commander with sets of instructions and ETAs for the barge. I also gave them a plan to follow-up with a 500-gallon collapsible-bag of water, sling-loaded with one of the first helicopters coming off the USS *Eisenhower* at daylight. I stayed up until delivery had occurred by

11

barge. Then, I searched the entire airport to thank the colonel again, knowing he had to still be there as we were under a no vehicular movement restriction, but he was nowhere to be found. I thanked God for sending a man as His angel of deliverance for me and the men of that company. Exhausted, I climbed to the upper floor of the terminal to catch some sleep while the mosquitoes feasted on me.

At the morning brigade staff meeting, I was deemed a hero (not literally). When I deflected to Colonel Turner, the Transportation unit liaison said they had no officer named Turner; that there was only one colonel in that unit in Haiti and he was in the harbor all night. He later confirmed to me from their log book that a Major Williams was the person who radioed them. I just shut up talking further, and silently thanked God for sending His angel in the form of a man. *(I had a front row seat and did not realize it.)

Bad News

About a week later, at age 31, Melissa was diagnosed with colon cancer. However, another episode occurred that has always nagged at me. I found out that the Red Cross and my Brigade Commander thought that I had refused to return to the U.S. Unless I had lost my mind, I was never part of that conversation. But that word got back to Melissa and hurt her badly. I was angry with the Red Cross and never got to the bottom of who said that I had refused to return to the U.S.

Thankfully, my Commander told me that his wife had informed him that the cancer was malignant and he was sending me home. I was grateful. The joy on Melissa's face to see me at her bedside when she woke up was worth so much to me – I did not know then that she had heard a report of me refusing to return. (Comment: Later, after I returned to Haiti, Melissa received a letter sent to Ft. Drum addressed to a Randy Williams that was not me. This may be the explanation for the Red Cross having crossed signals– it was meant for an enlisted man from a different unit who also deployed to Haiti. His girlfriend wrote in extremely graphic terms, according to Melissa. Melissa was stunned until she figured out that she and I were in Jordan during a rendezvous mentioned in the girlfriend's letter.)

I was to be with Melissa through recovery from the cancer removal and start of chemotherapy. Her mother, Betty, was with her when I got back, to which I was also grateful, as were our three sons. I think I learned to like Betty more as she stayed as long as she could. However, my duties as Brigade logistical officer would cause me to be ordered back to the island nation in early December (and sooner than any of us were ready to have happen). I then realized that life was fragile and that Betty and Melissa understood that far better than I.

Melissa's doctor told me that the cancer was stage 4; it had breached the colon and entered two lymph nodes. Melissa later told me that before I arrived, she was frightened for her young family. Our boys seemed so fragile, only ages 11, 9, and 5, at the time. She had prayed to God to allow her to see her sons grown. I wish now that I would have asked more details about God's response, but she only said that He would grant her request – I can say that God honored whatever pledge He gave her in that regard. We had nine very good years together and then two mostly distressing years. By God's grace, we saw our five-year old

We attended a formal military function in the spring of 1996, less than six months after ending a year of chemotherapy.

turn into a responsible 16-year-old without whose help I could not have made it those last two years.

The Return of Bad Times

We had been assigned to the U.S. Embassy in Kuwait from 2001-2003. It was a traumatic time with 9/11, the attacks against the Taliban/Al Qaeda forces from units in Kuwait, and then the invasion of Iraq. With all this, we still had time to help establish the American Embassy Chapel of Kuwait. While I was the first treasurer, I tip my hat to four others as the real visionaries of this effort. We also took time to visit Italy and Thailand – both were great vacations. However, Melissa began feeling something was wrong inside her body. She saw some U.S. military flight surgeons at Camp Doha, but they pooh-poohed her request for a laparoscopic procedure to find out the cause. They told her she did not know what she was asking for and that she suffered being a hypochondriac from the previous bout with cancer – in essence, they did nothing for her.

When we returned to U.S. Central Command in Tampa, Florida for my second tour there, the plan was to only spend a year there, then go to Yemen as the senior military officer for a one-year tour without family, due to safety concerns. On October 1, 2003, Melissa looked gorgeous in her purple Indian sari as we celebrated my promotion to colonel. Meanwhile, she had been seeking medical assistance at civilian hospitals to determine what was going on inside her. After a first test revealed nothing, she took a second, different test. On October 31st, she called me in tears to say, "It's happening all over again." A test revealed that both ovaries were grossly misshapen, and the doctors suspected that this was caused by cancer. She told me that Dr. Cohen had said that the colon cancer would come back in the female organs if it came back at all. We scheduled a hysterectomy for the first available date, November 13th (Friday the 13th at that).

Visions and Words Begin for Me

November 12, 2003. It was not much of a birthday for me; we went to bed worried about Melissa's surgery the next day to remove her ovaries. That night, I had one of the worst nightmares/visions of my life, although the details were fuzzy the next day. All around me seemed so black, and I could not find Melissa for most of it. When I did, I saw she was suffering. This replayed throughout that sleepless night. I prayed so hard for her, offering to give my life in exchange. I had this Voice in my head toward morning that told me that she would not survive this battle with cancer. I was not to tell her or anyone else how it would end but was to love and encourage her in the time she had left.

November 13th. The hysterectomy surgery/biopsy was like sleep walking. I knew what the doctor would report, and found Nina Radford (Melissa's close friend), her sister, Laura, and others were shocked at my calmness. Nina said she was certain that the issue would not be malignant cancer. I only told her I had nightmares without going into detail. Following the surgery, seeing Melissa with a colostomy bag for the first time caused me concern. I remembered how she had hated the scars from her previous surgery. I took a class at the hospital which trained me how to help her with the colostomy bag and with wound care.

November 2003-July 2004

This Chemo period was pure agony for Melissa. She ended up cutting it short. I remember being sent on several overseas missions when I felt I should have stayed. Thankfully, I had Nina and my son, Joshua, to depend upon to get Melissa to her appointments when I was away. When the surgeon implanted the port in her chest, I was reminded of the port in my younger brother's chest during his battle with leukemia – and the comment that few ever have the device removed. My brother, Ron, did not live to have it removed.

I believe it was in February of 2004 that we took Jonathan to a Christian concert with The News Boys, Rebecca St. James and a young guy named Jeremy Camp, as lead off act. During Jeremy's part, he spoke of losing his first wife to cancer and the long painful process, the periods of doubt, and the constant encouragement of his wife though she was wasting away. He wrote a beautiful song titled, "I Still Believe" from this tragic period. When he mentioned his wife's name was Melissa, I saw my Melissa crumble. She said that at that moment God told her she also would not survive this cancer. (Comment: Although we both had now heard the same message of death drawing near, we still hoped that God would change His mind. We attended several healing and prayer services at Church in our desperation.) She later asked that I play that song by Jeremy Camp at her funeral – for me.

At the end of April, I took her on a military trip to Tucson at the behest of a former great boss of mine and so I could get away and have her near me. When we returned, she and Nina went to Turtle Island – which she just gushed over – I was happy for that. Later, the Church helped me arrange a surprise celebration of the end of her chemotherapy. Kay Mills and Nina helped so much. I remember praying aloud at the event for another 40 years together and being chided by some of the older Church people because I was asking for such a short period – I smiled outwardly, but wanted to scream that we had so little time left.

In the summer, we attended a Chondra Pierce/Sandi Patti Concert with Nina. Melissa enjoyed this event so much and even won a tour jacket in the door prize raffle and just about danced up to the stage to receive it from Chondra. She looked so cute.

Melissa's Ministry Vision

In late December, during a dream, the Lord instructed me to support Melissa's ministry in all ways possible. Oddly, it had always been Melissa supporting me, except in her work with the Cubbies of the

AWANA programs. However, in my desperation, I hoped this meant she had a reprieve from the death sentence. I promised the Lord I would do my best. I told Melissa of this dream and we both wondered what it could mean.

Then in June 2004, Pastor Randall Hosea asked me to teach a Sunday School class for couples with no children. I was concerned that I could not give this effort the time it deserved because of caring for Melissa and my work. Melissa encouraged me in this, and, looking back, I am thankful that when I asked God to let me say no in good conscience, He did not allow me to do so. Besides Rick Matthews from our Sunday School class, I have had at least a dozen people tell me how Melissa's example impacted them and changed their lives. This class was her ministry, but I just didn't see it at the time.

Chemo Did Not Work This Time

At the end of July 2004, I went back to Iraq while Melissa was scheduled for more tests. The day I flew into Baghdad (part of the trip was with wounded soldiers we picked up at Tallil Air Base), Melissa informed me that the cancer was detected throughout her entire abdomen and that she was going to meet with a surgeon, Dr. Kelley, about an experimental treatment. She and Nina were also upset at the cold attitude of the oncologist in describing her situation.

Screaming into a Locker

I slept very little while in Baghdad, having Melissa constantly on my mind. One night (among many nights) when the sirens alerted us to incoming mortar or missile fire, I stood where I was, hoping to be struck by a mortar round rather than running for a bunker. In my misery, I went to an empty locker, stuck my head in it, and screamed in anger and hurt for God to help her. When I finished, I collapsed on the ground and asked God what I was to do. Again, I heard that I was to love her and

17

give her all the hope I could for the time I had left with her, and I was not to show her my despair. I did not believe I could handle such a mission, but I promised God I would try.

I was able to leave Iraq earlier than planned due to Melissa's condition. On the way out of Baghdad, August 13 (Friday the 13th again), our convoy from the Green Zone to Baghdad International Airport had to detour along the river due to an attack along the main road. When we got to the airport, we quickly got signed on with a C-130 heading to Qatar. After a few hours, we eventually lined up to get on the plane. I had just climbed the stairs to enter the plane when a large explosion shook us. I remember fire, heat, smoke and debris littering the runway. It appeared that a missile of some kind had hit the fuel bladders beside the plane – but I never learned exactly what occurred. We disembarked quickly and ran through the confused scene to a nearby bunker. The fire was eventually extinguished, the runway cleared, and the plane deemed airworthy, so we re-boarded quickly and flew out. I had again survived, but was not so sure I was happy for that until I considered how Melissa would have quickly given up the will to live without me.

Last Chance Operation by Dr. Kelley

When I returned, I met with the surgeon, Dr. Scott Kelley. He was a breath of hope and clarity. I also cut all connections with Melissa's oncologist and asked for a new one. I came to consider Dr. Kelley a friend. We arranged a radical procedure in late August that had shown promise with another kind of cancer. The surgeon would cut out all cancer he could find then subject the abdomen to a heated chemo bath. After the surgery, Dr. Kelley said there was a lump of cancer in the uterine area that could not be removed without damaging her urinary tract – this was so disappointing to me and the assembled family. The operation seemed to almost kill her from the great pain it inflicted. Recovery was slow, and it likely sped up the spread of the disease to her lungs. She was in much pain until November. She slept through much of September and October. I learned to give her a series of IVs through her port and care for her other needs. Also, I was asked to go through a pilot program on care-giving that focused on my training and mental health. The young man who was involved with teaching the program often found our faith to be a help that many did not have. This was a very worthwhile program for both of us.

A Voice from Above

Not long after the failure of the warm chemo bath to stem the growth of tumors, I found myself under great stress from a variety of sources, but mostly watching my wife losing her battle. My daily quiet times and running five miles seemed my only release. One day when working at MacDill AFB, I arrived very early for a long run, some crunches, and pushups. As I ran, my mind stayed mostly on Melissa's situation and prayers for her and my boys. As I finished a 6-mile route along the bay, I stopped a good distance from the locker room and, once again yelled, "God help me!" I immediately heard a strange voice yell back from somewhere above me, "It will be okay." I looked everywhere and saw no one who could have been the responder. I admit that I felt a thrill of excitement that stayed with me until I returned home and described the event to Melissa. Her kind eyes showed compassion for me as I asked what it could possibly mean. I then remembered that God looks at everything from the perspective of eternity and thought, "Well, His version of okay may look nothing like my version. How do I gain His perspective?"

It was so rare to see Melissa eat that I made her a promise that I would drive across the county to get anything that sounded good to her. It did not happen often, but the staff at Johnny Carino's in Zephyrhills and I became friends during this period. She did have an occasional taste for pasta, which I was glad to serve her.

In early December 2004, we selected a site in Riverview, Florida, and arranged a mortgage on that retirement house I had always promised her that she could choose. Financially, it seemed an unwise decision, but it was not just in keeping a promise. It gave her hope and a dream to focus on. I always felt that God smiled on this gesture.

Melissa knew this would be her last Christmas and asked that I buy her nothing. I immediately rebelled at the idea, but she insisted. She spoke of all the pretty things she had. After not being able to afford much during our first dozen years of marriage, we had accumulated many pretty things, especially jewelry. I remembered then that I had never bought her the set of diamond stud earrings she had always wanted. For Christmas, she got a set of those and a large jewelry armoire. I got grumbled at, but I saw the appreciation in her eyes. She busied herself with arranging her things in the armoire and only took off those earrings for her surgeries during her remaining days. I think she saw I had not given up on her, and she repeatedly told me how she loved those earrings.

In January 2005, Melissa told me of one night when she was feeling so unlovable due to the ugliness of the disease and alone in her pain, she prayed for God to help her and let her know He was out there. She said she suddenly felt a presence and warmth completely envelop her and she heard the words, "I do love you," and, "It will be okay." She was so excited when she told me of this.

Valentine's Day Punch in the Stomach

A gynecological specialist verified our fears that the cancer had now protruded into her vaginal area. Melissa took it so badly. "Happy Valentine's Day," is all she said as she sobbed on the way home. I was numb for her.

In late February or early March 2005, she had another operation to allow her to breathe because of the fluid preventing her right lung from expanding. She knew I spent much time with the Lord each morning, and sometime around this point, she asked me if the Lord had told me she would die. I knew the answer was yes, but the Lord had bidden me keep that from her, so I lied to my beloved. I am not certain she believed me. It is a regret I still carry. I was lying to myself too because I could not, at that time, see the ministry of hers that I was supposed to support.

While waiting for the results of our last routine scan at Moffitt Cancer Treatment Center in June of 2005, Melissa sat talking to a young woman and fawned over her four-month-old daughter in her lap. This 21-year-old woman was accompanied by her mother who cared for the baby while she went inside for testing. Melissa learned from the two women that the younger woman had inoperable brain cancer with a prognosis of six months to live. Her husband had left her because he couldn't "deal" with this tragedy. Melissa turned to me and quietly stated, "We have lived a very good life together." To which, I could only say, "Amen." It suddenly struck me, as I looked around that room where so many waited and expected bad results, that indeed there were a lot of people far worse off than us. We had lived a blessed life in so many wonderful ways these past 23 ½ years.

Build Her House

As I had to make decisions about the interior of the house, I had to go to the Lord during a quiet time and ask for wisdom on how to keep the house within my ability to afford. Once again, I had that Voice in my head that said, "Give her the house you promised her." I okayed all of the upgrades she wanted and began calling it Melissa's house. The look in her eyes when I ordered the granite counter tops was all the payment I needed to cover the cost. I remember coming home one day to find her polishing those counter tops and stepping back in pride, while she was just a scarecrow of a figure – I again knew it was the right decision.

The summer of 2005 was a blur between work and driving myself to finish her house. I do appreciate the help given by Melissa's family and our many Church friends. We were all rewarded one day when one of her favorite songs was playing on the stereo. She was walking from the kitchen and started bopping her head and doing a little dance to the music. Jonathan shouted, "Mom is getting her groove on," and she had the cutest smile. Despite the ravages of the cancer, we got to see her beauty shine from within (a memory I will cherish of this brave soul). I finished the house in mid-August, except some final touches, and felt like collapsing.

Many-Eyed Angel Vision

One morning in late August, Melissa awoke upset. She said she had the very real dream of an angel with eyes all over his body and wings that stood facing her. She said that he said nothing, but she knew he was telling her it was time to go. She said she started arguing with him that Randy and the boys still needed her, but the angel would not budge. She said that she then told the angel that she had to kiss Randy one last time before she went with him. We cried together. While ripping my heart, I saw in her description of her vision the feisty bride I had married almost 24 years previously. Imagine the audacity of arguing with a guardian of the throne room of God Himself.

I then had to stop going to my Sunday School class so I could be with her. She was so tired and did not like to be stared at. Graciously, my Sunday School class started meeting in our home on Sunday mornings. That meant a lot to Melissa. I give my thanks to Rick Matthews for organizing this.

During our final visit to the oncologist on August 31st, he delivered the news that the cancer had spread further and there was nothing more he could do for us and was recommending Hospice. We asked him for time alone so we could cry together before leaving that dreaded place one last time.

Despite this, I was still required to go to the Pentagon for a three-day bilateral meeting with some senior Arab military officers. I still have trouble forgiving the decision-maker behind this. However, my friend and colleague, Marine Colonel John Gauthier, covered for me when I returned so I could be with Melissa until she passed, plus an extra two weeks to help the boys and to get myself together. I certainly had plenty of unused leave accrued.

<u>Vision of "6"</u>

Melissa woke me one morning in early September and asked me for help with a vision she had. She kept having a replay of her running across a finish line with people in the grandstands and all around her on the track cheering, clapping and congratulating her. However, they were all wearing a large number "6" on their shirts, and she could see the number 6 on banners and posters throughout the stadium. She said she asked one of the cheering people what it meant, but they did not seem to hear her and just patted her on the back. Then the same dream re-played several more times. We could not figure it out. I later told Nina that I thought she might pass away on the 6th, but that turned out not to be.

Around the end of September, she had some terrible stomach aches and was in distress so I took her to the hospital at the advice of the Hospice nurse. Our hero, Dr. Kelley, came to check on her and run tests. He told me that her digestive system had shut down and that she would starve to death in under two weeks at this point. He asked if I wanted her hospitalized but I declined because I knew her place was in our home. He also let me know that the cancer had become so aggressive when it resurfaced in 2003 that little could have been done. The doctor informed me when I complained about this not being caught sooner when she sought help in Kuwait, that if we had operated sooner she possibly would have had a more miserable and likely shorter life. The next day she was shocked when I told her what the doctor said about how short her time was. After a moment, she was calm and stayed that way until death unless she heard a loud noise or something got close to her face.

At her sister Laura's request, I had the three boys sit and talk with her. At this point, they seemed to hide from the inevitable. Josh rarely poked his head out of his room. Jonathan played his piano, but did not speak much. Nathan did spend some time with her, but would disappear. I had to force myself to sit with her also. It was so hard to see her suffer in silence. She occasionally gave me a wry smile. Her eyes followed me, but she did not speak much.

The hardest part of her last two weeks was her pulling away from me. Hospice training had warned me of such, but it did not totally prepare me for the break in our relationship. My confidant, lover, friend, and advisor was suddenly gone. I was like a trusted servant that she depended on, and she was like a schoolmaster teaching me what I needed to understand. Most of the next two sections came from her during this time of pulling away.

Direction/Advice from Melissa in Her Last Days

"We left Nathan in Arkansas too long. I thought it would be good for him, but he has lost his way. Try to get him back on the right path. He knows what is right, but he has always hidden from us when he is doing wrong. He can be a good man like you." (He is on the right path in so many areas as of this moment in my writing.)

"Josh is a good guy down deep; do not give up on him. The light switch will come on and he will turn out okay." (Comment: I can bear witness that she was right.)

"Jonathan is bound for great things. Watch out for girls because they can derail him. He is sensitive and driven; girls see that and are attracted." She also pointed out girls not for Jonathan and said that when his wife-to-be comes along, "You will recognize her when you meet her." (I have no idea how she could have known that.)

"Don't decide to retire from the military until well after I am gone, you enjoy it so much."

"Do not abandon the boys." (This was my biggest struggle for several years.)

"Wear my rings around your neck on one of my gold chains so it is close to your heart." (I did so.)

"Don't get re-married in one year like my uncle." (In response to this, I promised to wear her wedding band for a year – it took me three years after her passing before I could remove it.)

Around October 12th, she shocked me by saying, "I want you to re-marry so you do not grow old alone."

"Don't spend time at the cemetery. I want you and the boys to remember me and how I was when I was healthy."

"Stay in contact with my family. MawMaw (her mom, Betty) will take this hard, and the boys need to stay connected with them."

Her Last Requests

Melissa requested no flowers at the funeral, just have people send money to the Church for dividing between the Food Pantry and the Single Mother's Ministry. (For weeks afterward, I had people tell me about the impact of her request. Over twenty families had a full Thanksgiving meal, and many women in need had clothes and other necessities provided.)

Do not allow her father to come to the funeral so as not to further upset her mother.

Have a closed casket so people could remember how she had been before the ravages of cancer.

She told me of several ministries she would have liked to have blessed and asked that I try to support as I could: Jeff and Sherri Butler trying to start a new Church in New York, Evangelist Randy Bane, and our home Church of FBCR, among others.

The Angel Returned and the Loss of My Beloved
(October 18, 2005)

She had breathed raggedly all night, and I feared each would be the last. Yet I knew her suffering would end soon, and that was good. At about 10:00 a.m., with only Nina in the room, she tried to talk but her throat was so dry and crackly that I could not make out the words. I held my ear near her mouth and made out that she was saying, "A man is there," indicating the foot of the bed. I asked if the angel with many eyes was there and she nodded yes. I told her that it was okay to go with him because God was waiting for her and we would be okay. She tried to say something else, but we could not understand her words (which I regret). She stopped trying to communicate because I could tell having my face close to hers was bothering her. She then got a determined look on her face and started shaking her head no. About two minutes later she became still, and I could sense that her spirit was departing, so I leaned over and kissed her one last time because I knew she could not come back for me. I only hope she knew what I had done since this was her last communication. Yet, somehow I knew then and still know now, that she left her peace on our family and her house.

Her heart finally stopped at about 4:10 p.m. I said silently, "The Lord giveth, and the Lord taketh away," then aloud, "Blessed be the Name of the Lord." I took off her diamond stud earrings as she had requested me to do. After cleaning her up, I sat in stunned awe of what had occurred, as my sons and family came in. When I went outside to see her body transferred to the funeral parlor hearse, I remember how bright and mockingly beautiful the day was – clear and blue.

I sat at the computer and tried to compose an e-mail to inform friends of her passing, only to discover two weeks later that the e-mail had never gone out – my mind was not working well. I took two of her Ambien and slept for 13 hours straight.

Up until the day she died, Melissa had convinced herself that God would miraculously heal her. On October 17th, her kidneys failed and she could not control bodily functions. I will say that I had little to no sleep for those last two days. Surprisingly, she had walked herself to the bathroom that morning – I do not know where her physical strength came from. I also do not remember who had been under my roof, other than Nina occasionally telling me to eat. (Nina later said that Melissa asked her to come just to look after me – what else could I say about her wisdom.) I learned later that Kim Walliser had slept in my home just to help. To say Melissa was brave throughout this ordeal would be a woeful lack of accuracy. I had seen no warrior in my over 25 years of military service who came close. She spent much of her time worried about the impact on her family rather than herself. She did her very best to make her parting as easy on us as humanly possible.

Funeral

Again, my church family and Nina stood by us. Pastor Keathly assisted me with funeral details and dealt with difficult family members over Melissa's last requests so as to protect her mother. Our former Youth Pastor, Billy Hodges, brightened my life by finding a video of him singing a duet with Melissa back in 2000. We played this song, "Jesus Saves" at her funeral so all could see how healthy, beautiful (inside and out), and talented she was. The lyrics of the song were a fitting testimony of her life. The Easters family put together a really beautiful picture montage set to music. Nina signed one of Melissa's favorite songs. Becky, Melissa's younger sister, read a tribute to her hero - that meant a lot to me. For her funeral, I felt compelled to speak. I still cannot say why, but I could not let someone who did not know her as I did say the final words over her body. We played the two songs she requested, "I Still Believe" by Jeremy Camp and "I Can Only Imagine" by MercyMe. I think she was dancing along with the lyrics.

Whenever I had the awful, yet sacred duty to officiate over a funeral for a fallen service member during my military career, my usual stoicism broke down at a specific point. This occurred as I knelt and recited the "On behalf of a grateful nation" speech as I looked into the sad eyes of a wife and handed her the folded flag from her husband's coffin. My eyes just leaked. Well, my eyes leaked often that day, and sometimes without warning over the next several months.

Advice to Caregivers and Those Who Have Lost Loved Ones
(particularly after battles with cancer or another prolonged illness)

The Psalmist wrote,
"Why are you in despair, O my soul?
And why have you become disturbed within me?
Hope in God, for I SHALL AGAIN praise Him
for the help of His presence."
Psalms 42:5 (NASB)

I want to pause in this story to salute all those caregivers out there. I know your struggles and wish to share some things that, along with my faith in God, allowed me to maintain sanity and be helpful to my patient. It is my hope some of these may help you as well.

Looking back, one of the smartest things I did after we learned that Melissa's colon cancer had returned, was to sign up for a pilot program for caregivers at Moffitt Cancer Center. I learned to administer drugs and nutrition via pick lines, use heparin to clean tubing, dress wounds, and change colostomy bags. But I was also taught how to take care of myself so I wouldn't lose focus or become nonfunctional as a caregiver. Later, when my second wife, Sharon, was diagnosed with pancreatic cancer and we evacuated her from Kuwait, I tried to pass on these lessons to our daughter, Rachel, to help her cope until I could return to assist with Sharon.

From the Moffitt Cancer Center lessons, I found my keys for remaining stable were: **prayer, exercise, eating right, getting rest,** and **arranging with family, friends, or a hospice nurse to take short breaks**. I was blessed to have Melissa's close friend, Nina Radford, and then daughter Rachel in the two long fights against cancer. Church friends and colleagues also provided assistance of many kinds, to include food and socialization. I owe a great debt to Kim Walliser, Kay Mills, and Kathy Hosea of First Baptist Church of Riverview, Florida for their undying devotion to our Lord and their friend Melissa as the days drew to a close in her earthly pilgrimage.

If you feel like you no longer have the strength to go on, God can give you strength way beyond what you think you could ever bear. At times, I felt my strength and resolve ebbing due to the daily grind of suffering that I witnessed. Yet, each time I prayed to Jesus to give me strength to make it through another day, or hour, or sometimes just another cruel moment, I found that I could keep going. For those of faith, I recommend you keep that prayer line of communication open constantly throughout the day. It is okay to get mad at God or even to vent your hurt toward Him. He is big enough to handle it. He saw me through many dark moments so I did not lose patience with others or fail to calmly face any situation. I must add Christ at the top of my list to thank for never leaving me alone and for galvanizing my faith in these fiery trials.

Chapter 2: Grief and a Call to Ministry

"As the rain and the snow come down from heaven, and do not return to it without watering the earth and making it bud and flourish, so that it yields seed for the sower and bread for the eater, so is my word that goes out from my mouth: It will not return to me empty, but will accomplish what I desire and achieve the purpose for which I sent it." Isaiah 55:10-11 (NIV)

Mourning Period

Black

I had no vision of the future, unlike my usual self. When I remembered the Holy Spirit saying, "It will be okay," I now heard it in a mocking tone. I spent time with the boys when I could and used the additional weeks off to help Jonathan with his driver's test, his first job, and to open a bank account. For weeks afterward, I sat in our dining room listening to music, mostly Selah and Melissa's favorites. I put together every jigsaw puzzle we owned – some twice. I told the boys not to blame themselves because they were innocent of what God had seen fit to do with their mom. Inwardly, I wondered if I, as spiritual leader of the family, had been partly to blame. I had agreed with Melissa to allow her to choose our place of retirement after all those years of following me, rather than ask God where He wanted me to be and what He wanted me to do at this time in life.

Advice to the Church and Other Pools of Friends

Being widowed does not make a person bad or predatory. Don't disassociate from us because our marital status changes. You harm our recovery.

Don't invite us to join your singles group one week after burying a spouse, as happened to me. We should neither be viewed as a pariah nor a meat selection at the local butcher shop. You can drive good people away. I must think it works the same for those who lose a spouse in other ways.

Advice to Those in Mourning

Expect people to say stupid or hurtful things. I don't really think they mean to do so, but some feel like they have to say something.

Expect some member of the family to make strange (and hurtful) requests about stuff that belonged to your loved one. I wish I had good advice on how best to deal with this, but alas, I can only warn you in advance.

The best advice that I failed to follow during this time came from Pastor Randall Hosea. He told me not to try being mother and father, but just be dad to my boys. I think I confused them that first Christmas as I tried to do the things that their mother had previously done, as I sat back and watched. It took me a few years to realize this, and make a course correction. So, I pass that on to any who lose a spouse while having young children at home.

You will need space to mourn privately throughout the day. I am not normally a crier, and I hate to burden others with my pain, although I did learn that I needed to do so at times. When I returned to work at U.S. Central Command, I used a green-shaded lamp that had been in my office from my first day, but that I had never lit. I told my subordinates that if the green-shaded light was on, do not approach unless it was a matter of life or limb, or a general required me. They honored this request. There were moments that tears just ran down my face as I tried to do my work. It is okay to set up some kind of "green-shaded lamp" in your life so well-meaning folks don't intrude on those moments when you just need to be alone.

Advice for Those Wishing to Show Sympathy

Just know that nothing you can say will heal that broken heart. I noticed that those who showed greatest compassion just came and sat beside me silently while not trying to explain why God allowed this to occur or give me a way to think about it. Just be there. Don't ask me what I need; you might not like a truthful response. If you bring something useful for me or my family and just spend time, you will have blessed us as much as is humanly possible.

Change of Careers

I had started to retire in August, but Melissa prevented me. After her death, before returning to work, I had several quiet times with the Lord about this matter. God revealed to me that I yet had some work left at CENTCOM in showing my colleagues how a Christian was to live despite loss. His plans did require me to retire and be available to His call. I had no clarity of future purpose, but I had complete peace about retiring. As soon as I returned to work, I submitted my retirement request. However, it took several months for the Army to approve my retirement. This gave me almost a year to model living as a Christian for my military associates.

The Note

On December 5, 2005, I was traveling from Al Ain, UAE to Abu Dhabi to attend a meeting, then head for Riyadh, Saudi Arabia. I suddenly thought of calling an old friend in Kuwait since I would stop in there shortly on the way home. As I dug through my wallet for his business card, I found a note that Melissa had hidden there sometime in the past. (She often hid love notes in my bags when I left on missions.) I must have missed this one. Yet, that day would have been our 24th anniversary, and I got to hear from her again. It read:

My Dearest Love,

How hard it's been to let you go. I love you so much, and ache with loneliness already. Please, please take care of yourself. We (she meant the children and her, but I read this as Melissa and her heavenly friends) *will lift your name in prayer every day. Think of me often and know I love you more than anything. How I wish I could express it to you. Take care, my love.*

Yours forever,

Softy (this was my pet name for her)

I cried silently as I sat next to a burly major, who was also a Ranger, and he never knew. It was amazing that I had found that note on this day of all days. I do not know when she wrote it or hid it in my wallet. I continue to carry that note with me and I think of her often. It may seem that I was becoming a cry baby, but don't let that fool you. I was deadly serious and took risk with my life on occasion.

Melissa's Ministry Continued

During the first two weeks of December, a check for over $100,000 arrived from a military insurance plan that covered Melissa. I did not realize I had this coverage until weeks after her passing. I remember sitting in stunned silence looking at the check and asking God what He wanted me to do with it. In my budget, it became listed as "Melissa's Gift." God led me to give liberally to the pastor in New York, the Evangelist in North Carolina, a Pastor in Germany and toward a sudden, unexpected need at First Baptist Church of Riverview. I was also now able to cover the expenses of finishing the house the way Melissa wanted it. I also put money aside for Jonathan's college in case anything happened to me overseas as I went in and out of danger zones.

Two of the above-mentioned men of God called to tell me how Melissa had kept in touch and prayed for their ministries. I was not fully aware of the extent of her prayer assistance – she had never given money, but okayed the few small gifts I had sent their way previously.

The unexpected amount of money that arrived from Melissa's Gift had been enough to prevent one pastor from closing his doors and the other from turning down costly health insurance because of a lack of funds when he knew his wife and daughter would need treatment in the coming quarter. I cried again, then smiled, and stood in awe of what God had done through guiding my hand in a checkbook, trying to honor my wife's requests. *(Once again, I had a front row seat to see wonders that I just did not see coming.)

I credit the following to Melissa as well: I had a subordinate officer come to me in tears about his wife leaving him the day after Christmas and taking his children too. His family said to divorce her and that they could easily find a younger, better wife for him. But he loved his wife. I could tell by the way he spoke highly of her before this occurred. I remember thinking of Melissa and how the cancer had ruined her hormonal system and caused her to react uncharacteristically at times. I advised the fellow accordingly. He contacted her doctor and was patient with his wife. She eventually returned home and was devastated by what she had done. Shortly afterward, her doctor started hormone therapy, and she was her old self again. They now both think of me as their hero. I have explained that it was not me but lessons from God, taught to me by Melissa.

A New Direction

After a stint of visits to the Middle East on a variety of missions in the spring, I returned home. Then, during May 11-12, 2006, I heard God clearly calling to me, "Go to Kuwait." This was repeated during quiet times and sometimes during the day, and I became unsettled in my mind. I had no job prospects there, and I had not even created a resume` at this point, so I dismissed the matter by saying to the Lord in my quiet time on the 13th, "I can only go if You open the door, but I will obey." The Voice ceased for my next three quiet times.

Then, on May 16, 2006, and in short order, I received two e-mails from a retired general officer I had known in Kuwait. Unbeknownst to me, our dear friends, Talal Othman and Katherine Baker from the assignment in Kuwait, had told him of Melissa's passing and my plan to leave the Army. His first e-mail included a condolence and an offer for assistance in finding a job with his current company after my retirement. I need only send him my resume`. The Company (MPRI at that time) had jobs for military professionals in many places. His second email contained the following question:

Would you be interested in taking my job as the Program Manager here in Kuwait if you could bring your family?? It is a far out thought but it just might work. What is the date you would want to start work??

I was floored with how quickly God had opened the door for me to respond to His calling. Hence, I pursued the potential job in Kuwait. This would address all of my financial needs and allow me to pursue whatever spiritual mission God planned for me. However, I would not be able to take my boys.

Over the next few weeks, I asked the Lord for guidance on what spiritual mission He had for me in Kuwait. Many weeks later, I received the short answer, "Lead my people." That was a scary thought as I had not yet considered becoming a pastor or missionary. It was not until 2009 that I felt the call to be a pastor (as my mother-in-law, Betty, had always said would happen).

Music from Above

I awoke on June 1, 2006, Melissa's birthday, after a restless night of wrestling with the idea of abandoning the boys in pursuit of this mission from God. I admit that I was a bit down that day. My coffee maker had beeped notifying me that the first cup was ready. As I started to pour that first cup, I suddenly heard the tinkling of music. As I looked around, I found that it came from up above the kitchen cabinets where some of

Melissa's "Noah's Ark" music boxes were placed a year earlier. I listened closely and could hear "How Great Thou Art" playing. I tried to sense a spiritual presence because this occurrence was beyond logic, but I felt absolutely nothing. I took a ladder and checked the box that had played. The uniformly thin layer of dust showed it had not been touched in many months. I asked each of the boys later and all swore to have never touched it. While I cannot be certain why it picked that day and time to suddenly play, it was a reminder to me that Melissa was busy praising God in heaven and that I needed to obey the Master of the universe and stop worrying about what might or might not happen. I will ponder this for some time to come. Other than a comfort to me, I cannot fathom any other meaning to this event.

I will spare any readers the story of my last few weeks at CENTCOM. I will say, however, that I worked with some outstanding officers and NCOs. I had a superb retirement ceremony, hosted by an Australian Commodore, that I found fitting in all respects. Kay Mills and my church family put on a retirement party for me that was really enjoyable and included many dear friends. My church family had designed a map spoofing 'Where in the World is Carmen San Diego?' which showed all the countries of the world where they thought I had worked. Little did they know which spots they had missed due to military confidentiality.

Wrong College?

In August of 2006, Jonathan and I were trying to make decisions about his college career. In June, he had given his life to the Lord and felt a call into church music ministry. (I also discovered that he had continued to blame himself for his mother's death – a natural tendency, but clearly wrong.) We visited the campus of Southeastern University, associated with Assemblies of God and Pentecostal groups, though attended by Baptists and other denominations. While there, the Spirit kept whispering in my ear that this was the place. I asked Jonathan his thoughts on the college and he confirmed what the Spirit had already revealed to me. We have been questioned by my Baptist colleagues about this decision. I sometimes questioned it myself at that time, but I think he received an excellent education and certainly finished with finely-honed musical skills.

In late August and September, Jonathan and I kept some promises made to Melissa to visit friends in Italy and go to Hawaii. During this period, I was finally hired by MPRI for the Kuwait job, although I saw it as a done deal in God's eyes. The wrestling match I faced from that point was how to keep my promise to Melissa not to abandon the boys. I would take care of them as best I could, but I felt that disobeying my Lord would cause them greater harm. I began work on October 1st in Alexandria, VA, and visited Kuwait to prepare for the transition.

Jonathan's Storm
(December 2006)

In late November and early December, I had a series of visions of Jonathan at sea in a storm, and I could not get to him – darkness, strong winds, and lightning buffeted me so I could get no closer. The Spirit's message was that the only way I could help him was to pray for him, send him advice, and provide for his physical needs. He would have to weather this storm without me, and only with advisors of his own choosing. When I returned home in December, I told Jonathan of this, and said that he must be on his guard.

In late December, I was awakened by a dream and a Voice. This dream was of Jonathan and a young girl from church walking, holding hands. The Voice then said, "Stop it or health will be affected." I awoke with a start, prayed for understanding, and asked God to show me a sign that this was true. Immediately my phone rang, although it was not yet 5:30 a.m. It was Pastor Randall's cell phone, but there was no one there. I tried to call him back, but received no answer. Later, he returned my call and laughed about dropping his phone while getting ready for his morning walk. I asked for an appointment to talk to him about a dream I had had.

After talking to Pastor Randall, I pulled Jonathan aside and told him to knock it off with this specific girl. I explained how Mom wanted him to watch out for girls and not commit to marriage until his schooling was finished. I tried to explain to him about my extended family and how early relationships by young people unprepared for life and out-of-wedlock births had caused pain and resentment. My culture from the Ozarks promoted early marriage and out-of-wedlock pregnancies. I also informed him that he could not be true to his mother's direction to finish college before getting serious with a girl; however, I did not tell him that this was one girl that Melissa said was not for Jonathan, nor about my dream that morning. He became angry and started yelling at me. I told him that his mother said that God was still preparing a special girl for him and that, according to his mother, I would recognize her as such when I met her one day. I also informed him that God had told me that, if Jonathan was true to his commitment, then the right girl would be as special as his mother, beautiful on the inside and outside—maybe more so.

Jonathan reacted badly and told many people, including this girl's family, about our discussion but it came across as a racial issue. While I was disappointed in Jonathan's reaction, I knew he was young and with a big hole in his life, like me. Perhaps he sought to fill the void caused by his mother's passing with a romance. During my quiet times, I sensed God telling me that I should not defend myself with anyone, including the girl's family.

While I found that prompting strange, I followed it as I met with the girl's family and then the Youth Pastor after our next church service. The parents thought I was teaching racial hatred. I don't think they heard my explanation of my own culture tending toward early marriages and out-of-wedlock births. They did not know my family was currently dealing with this very issue. A young man in our family, who had not finished his college education and did not have a good job, had a pregnant girlfriend. I dearly loved that family and their girls, but I fear we will never be friends again. The Spirit has again said that He will take care of that. I will admit that I was unsure of Jonathan's relationship with the girl after that day. When he later told me that she had a health crisis that they could not figure out and almost lost her, I hurt inside, feeling I had failed to prevent it. The Spirit did not say whose health would suffer harm.

(Note: I can say in the year 2013, I met the girl Melissa said I would meet and I performed her wedding to my son, Jonathan, on December 10, 2016.)

A Change of Venue

In January 2007, I arrived in Kuwait for duty along the Iraqi border. It was a backside of the desert time for me to contemplate life (like Moses when he fled Egypt and tended sheep for a time). I was not in a position to serve in a church, but the group I worked with was seriously troubled and I feel I provided some stable leadership. In mid-March, I moved to a position in Kuwait City and began attending the American Embassy Chapel of Kuwait (AECK) that Melissa and I had been founding members of back in 2002.

On my second visit, Pastor David Peacock approached me about becoming the Chairman of the Church Council, responsible for arranging all points of service and Sunday School, except the preaching. He mentioned there was some kind of difficulty in the Council that needed leadership. I looked at him in shock and said I only knew two people out of the 60 or so in the congregation. However, this was in line with what I was sent there for, so I said I would pray about it. Like my Sunday School class experience in 2004, the Lord did not let me say no. I was voted in as Chairman in April and immediately found that the Chapel had not submitted any IRS filings since its establishment – so I had immediate work to do of a mundane nature as well.

Answer to the Riddle of "6"
(May 2007)

In keeping a promise to Jonathan, I returned to speak at his high school graduation. The night before the graduation, I lay in bed and wrestled over what to say on Jonathan's behalf. I thought of Melissa and what she had said of him and how he was special. I then asked God for a word from Melissa that I could give Jonathan. God's response surprised me. I heard the same Voice I attribute to the Spirit of God say, "She brought six into the Kingdom, but one of those will bring in 60." In shock, I asked, "Is it Jonathan?" but got no reply. I thought again of Melissa's vision of "6" and now understood that over 1 ½ years after she received that vision, I had been given the interpretation. I do not know who the six persons are that Melissa led into the Kingdom. She had impacted so many lives, it is impossible to say, but in my heart, that promise of 60 is tied to Jonathan if he remains faithful.

I shared this with Nina but did not share it with Jonathan due to the pressure it would place on him. God gave me other words for Jonathan. I remember Melissa bemoaning that her time on earth was so short and that she had made no lasting impact. I thought how wrong she was and focused my speech on Jonathan being one part of her living legacy. I believe that vision was sent as an answer to her concern of having no impact. I see her being welcomed into the Kingdom of God by these many people who are celebrating her being responsible for bringing six other people into the Kingdom. I was too dense at the time to understand; it is now a point of awe with me. *(I had a front row seat.)

I also ended up acting as a witness at Nathan, my oldest son, and Monica's wedding. I then got to hold my first grandchild, Ethan, before returning to Kuwait.

Monica's Bout with Cancer

In early 2007, doctors discovered three lumps in my daughter-in-law Monica's breasts. A later test revealed precancerous cells in one lump, including the assumption that cancerous cells existed nearby. However, nothing could be done because Monica was pregnant at the time. After their son, Ethan, was born, she was immediately scheduled for a lumpectomy and a biopsy. Having just lost my wife, I prayed hard that God would spare her and Nathan this pain. Just before the surgery, the Lord laid on my heart to fast and pray for her if I truly wanted to see her healed.

On the day of her surgery and on the day the results were due back, I did fast and pray. It was awkward with the Kuwaitis. When I refused their offerings of refreshment due to fasting, they asked if I was Muslim. I replied no and that, as a Christian, I should not be telling them I was fasting, but I wanted to explain the reason for turning down their hospitality. Some of them replied that my fasting for someone on another continent made no sense and that I could eat anyway. "God would not mind," they insisted.

Later, when Nathan told me that the tests revealed no cancer or even precancerous cells, I jumped for joy and fell on my carpet (the normal prostrate place of prayer for me) to praise God. When I reported to the Kuwaitis about the answer to my prayer, they were impressed with my God. I had one of them ask me to pray for his relative a week later, and thankfully, that relative recovered.

Prayer for Vision

When I took up the duties as Chairman of the Chapel and began auditing five years of Chapel financial information, I discovered the Chapel had no real ongoing ministry in Kuwait other than to meet and distribute money to causes around the world. The one exception was a Christmastime gift to abused maids at other Embassy shelters. Many of the past volunteer Council members had stepped down over issues within the Council. I assume that is why I was asked to take up the mantle. The Chapel had a few members with spiritual depth. We were losing most of those with the summer turn-over. The Chapel had a set of bylaws but no real vision. I prayed for that vision. God showed me that the Chapel needed discipleship for deeper Christian development and opportunities to serve locally, rather than just sending funds elsewhere on the globe.

Pastor Randall's Visit - Filipina Maids Ministry

As I maintained contact with Pastor Randall of First Baptist Church of Riverview, Florida, (FBCR) about my boys, I learned that his initial plans for a summer sabbatical had fallen through. I knew that our church would lack a pastor for a month, so I asked Pastor Randall to come to Kuwait to fill this role. I was surprised that he accepted the opportunity and more surprised when The Lighthouse Church (TLC), a part of the New Evangelical Church of Kuwait, agreed to allow him to preach for our chapel and for their other services as well.

While in Kuwait, Pastor Randall opened doors of opportunity for the American Embassy Chapel (AECK) by preaching to abused maids who had sought refuge at the Philippine Labor Office. I saw the abused maids at the Philippine, Sri Lankan, and Indonesian Embassies as possible opportunities for local ministry.

While Pastor Randall preached, I became acquainted with the situation and needs of these ladies. It struck me to the heart. Later that day, at the Embassy Chapel, I pledged to work along with Pastor Martin of the TLC to help relieve some of the Embassy maids' burdens. In response, we provided several thousand dollars of toiletries, clothes, sleeping mats, and food.

Over the next six months, I attended all but three Friday early morning services. Regrettably, the Embassy maids received little support from the AECK. Linda Wallace of that congregation took over the Philippine Refuge ministry for me and proved herself a worthy ministry partner. That was a bright spot for me. While I continued helping her with supplies, I found my niche in preaching each time I visited the maids at the embassy, per Pastor Martin's request. We saw so many souls saved that I know this was a very good effort.

Because of constant turnover at the embassies, each week 10% of my audience would hear me for the first time. The Lord always gave me a word for them. Even at my lowest time (during the MPRI contract re-negotiation when I thought I would return to the U.S.), the Lord showed me that I was not done supporting those poor downcast souls at what we called the Filipina Mission.

Several non-Chapel folks gave generously to this cause, which uplifted me. The AECK agreed to take a collection to provide toiletry gift baskets to all three Embassies' abused maids at Christmastime. Since I would spend a month at Christmas in the U.S. visiting my sons, I wanted some tangible gift to show the ladies that they were not forgotten. Their needs were so great and continual, but we needed to do what we could. Even though I was not able to get AECK on board with establishing this as an ongoing ministry, I had found a compelling ministry for myself and Linda. She could do so much more for them than I, even a simple yet significant thing like giving them a hug.

Remove the Ring

In early September 2007, while I was having my quiet time, I was playing with my wedding ring on my right hand. I heard the Voice again. This time it said, "Take off the ring." Now, I had remained celibate as a widower, and no particular woman had been of any great interest to me, so this word seemed strange. I asked the Lord to allow me to continue wearing it until I went home in December. I heard no response from God, so I continued to wear the ring. In Kuwait, I wore the ring on my right hand. In that culture, this showed that I was promised to another – kind of fitting. If the Lord was preparing someone else for me, I was unaware. I did fear the impact of any new relationship on my sons and on my mother-in-law, Betty. Earlier that year, Betty had indicated that she would be mad at me if I remarried—despite Melissa having told me to remarry someday.

<u>Can I Go Home Now?</u>

I became the MPRI Program Manager on October 1st. Two days later, the Kuwait National Guard failed to come up with the money to maintain the MPRI contract. It appeared I was going home. The boys seemed to be doing poorly, so I felt the pull to return home. My employees, the Filipina Maids, and, to an extent, the AECK needed me there. I spent much time on the floor of my study in prayer, crying out for direction and seeking an answer, but none came for two very difficult weeks. I informed my sons, Pastor Randall, Pastor Dave and Linda that it looked as though I would be going home. I would know for certain by the next Thursday, October 18th, the second anniversary of my beloved's passing.

This coincided with the breaking of the fast of Ramadan, making for a long weekend. That Tuesday morning, I was directed by my company officials to inform the KNG that MPRI could not fulfill the contract demands for the money offered. After my morning coffee and scripture reading, I assumed my place on my rug to pray. I prayed that the Lord would direct me and show me His will. The Voice returned, saying, "Watch today, and you will see. You need do nothing but watch," and I finally felt a peace settle in my heart.

Three things occurred that day. First, after laying out the only way to give the KNG what they wanted, the KNG Military leader told me that I could be as flexible in performing the contract as I needed. However, he needed MPRI to stay in Kuwait and there would be no complaints about our doing what they wanted in a different way. Next, I got a call from a Chapel member that the senior Air Force Chaplain in Kuwait wanted to talk to me about taking up a collection for the Filipina Mission. Then, one of the senior MPRI officials signaled a willingness to consider the KNG proposals if I could show them that I could make it work. *(I had a front row seat.)

I spent a painful and tedious day convincing several key company officials of the wisdom in keeping MPRI in Kuwait. On Thursday, I had expected to be focusing on mourning Melissa's death and worries about my sons, but the Voice returned, telling me, "You will serve me here two more years." I was filled with a sense of peace which left no room for mourning. I then asked God, "What then? Could I return to Riverview?" I heard only silence in response to that question.

That day, the company president approved my modified plan and the KNG provided an acceptance document extending the contract until signatures on the new contract were completed. I was reminded of two years prior, the clear and beautiful sky, amidst a deep, personal struggle. My heart told me I needed to be in Riverview with the boys, but the Lord overruled this. In my sermon to the Filipinas the next day, I told the ladies that I was staying. From this, I was shown that God loved the maids and that I got more done when I shut up and listened to God so that He could accomplish His will.

Hope Within the Council

After a particularly bad Council meeting on October 26th, I felt compelled to confront the one member on the council who had withstood my attempts to get the AECK more involved with the Maids' ministries. Although I was suffering from a sinus infection and did not feel like arguing, I arranged to meet this gentleman for coffee near where we both worked. I prayed often through the day to have the right attitude. I felt the Spirit tell me to follow the words found in Matthew 18:15-17, and He would make a way to solve the relationship issues. I felt defeated as I sat down to drink coffee and chat, but the council member surprisingly took an apologetic stance. We had a good long discussion, and I felt that we might be able to work together from that point forward.

In November, the Council also voted to support the Chinese Home Church with a special offering. However, Pastor Dave met me for coffee later to share Pastor Jerry's (senior pastor at the TLC) concerns about that ethnic church's pastor having a history of not handling funds properly. Due to these concerns, the Chinese Home Church was no longer the primary ethnic church receiving weekly funds from TLC. I told him that unless there was a serious matter he could describe, I was constrained to carry out the wishes of the Council. Also, I had learned that this Home Church would have mixed monies anyway, since they regularly provided refreshments and, sometimes, a lunch for all who attended. This was always funded to some degree from their own personal budget. I offered to split the amount into monthly allotments to allay some concerns. This seemed like an odd conversation at the time. Later, it became clear that I had entirely missed the warning.

Maids Mission

The Lord continued to bless the Filipina Mission effort. We saw dozens saved over the first few months, and I was getting plenty of practice at preaching, despite how unlikely a preacher I may have been. At one service in December, five women claimed to have received Christ at the conclusion of my sermon and another two during Pastor Martin's following sermon. On my last day before travel back to the States, we collected money and supplies to provide Christmas gift baskets for 850 ladies, including maids at the Indonesian and Sri Lankan embassies, the Filipina ministry, and ladies of various ethnic groups in prison.

Frustration mounted as I gathered supplies for more than 850 women myself. The person who was supposed to do this did not complete the task. If it was going to happen, I would have to do it myself. I complained to God that this would not have happened if Melissa had been at my side; she would have taken on the task with me. I felt the Spirit respond by saying, "That is right, and that is why you need a helper alongside you." He did not remind me to take off my wedding ring, but I expected that at any moment.

The IRS Does Have a Heart

After struggling through the process of filing three years of delinquent IRS reports, promising to never be late again, and paying over $3,000 for the first of those fines, I received a bill of similar amount for the second delinquent filing. As it was year's end and the Chapel bylaws required us to grant all funds above $5,000, the Council had already voted to disburse those funds. I wrote the IRS requesting a delay in paying the second and third years' fines so we could properly provide Christmas gifts of toiletries, candy, and sweaters for 890 people in refuge at the Indonesian, Sri Lankan, and Philippine Embassies, as well as the Chinese Home Church. While awaiting that response, we went ahead with the purchases. To my surprise, a letter from the IRS in Ogden, Utah arrived in January. It cleared us of all penalties and included a check, returning our first penalty amount and three months of accrued interest on that penalty. I had what the old-time preachers called a shouting spell of hallelujahs. *(Again, I had a front row seat.)

Interlude

At this juncture in my story, I can say with all conviction that I was not at all comfortable with where I was or with what I was doing. I felt like I was muddling along in my ministry roles. Certainly, I owed a great debt to many people, especially the Foleys and the Hoseas who watched over my children in Florida. The church in Riverview had been a rock I could depend on. I intended to serve there one day, Lord willing. Folks from church and colleagues from MacDill AFB were tremendously helpful during the time of Melissa's passing. Words cannot express our gratitude for all the food, well-wishes, and visits we received during that time. And yes, I still cried at times when I thought of my beloved, but I had changed much.

Serving Melissa those two years taught me to serve at a level I had not known. Five years ago, I would never have considered buying cases of feminine hygiene products or women's underwear. Yet now, I easily shrugged off any comments by my colleagues about having an SUV full of both as I arranged delivery for the needed items. I thought nothing of anointing and praying for those young women, yet I would have never done that before. The Lord softened my heart to see needs and find a way to fill them. My quiet times, memories of Melissa, and thoughts about what she would do all gave me direction to serve the Filipinas. Otherwise, I felt I was a really bad fit. I know Melissa would have waded into the crowd of young ladies and loved on them, and cried and prayed with them. It was not appropriate for me to do so, and I had just recently started moving among them to shake a hand or touch a shoulder and say a blessing over them. I was horrified at the thought of scaring them after what some of them had been through at the hands of men in Kuwait.

On January 16, 2008, after three failed attempts, I finally took off my wedding ring. The next week, I removed the chain with Melissa's rings and stored them away, not certain what I should do with them. It had been very hard to put those tokens away, and I felt at times like I was being unfaithful to Melissa. That feeling tapered, but I was still uncertain if I was ready for a new relationship. However, the loneliness had become oppressive at times. I had two fears in this regard: being unequally yoked, and potentially missing God's best for me.

Commentary/Concern

I know I have not compiled every word received of the Spirit over these four years. There have been many other areas where the Lord had led me that I cannot recall or that do not seem connected to what is above – such as dealing with difficult people at work and church, financial matters, etc. It seems so much is hidden from me. I might easily have misinterpreted some of what I have explained. I am prepared to be wrong and can only pray that no one suffers harm from my error. A lingering question I have is, *if it took me 1 ½ years to understand the Vision of "6"* (and it now seems so clear*), what else am I misunderstanding yet acting upon as if it were clear?*

Third Anniversary of Melissa's Passing
(October 18, 2008)

I put my ring back on and again wore the chain with her rings. It came to my mind to fast and pray this day seeking direction and answers to so many questions. As I wrote this, I was still awaiting a response from God; however, I felt led to deliver some food items to my friends at the Chinese Home Church. During my return, the local radio played the James Blunt song "I'll Carry You Home" that got my attention. When I arrived to resume my prayer, I played Melissa's songs from her funeral. Yes, I clouded up pretty badly. I then was directed to pick up this project of writing again, though I do not know why.

Back in April of 2008, Pastor Jeff Butler and his dear wife and friend to Melissa, Sherri, came to Kuwait for ministry with me. I simply played a support role. They worked with the Filipinas, Chinese Home Church, and met a wonderful laborer of God, named Sriyani Premadosa. Sriyani was in their service to the Sri Lankans of the Rooftop Ministry (foreigners illegally living in Kuwait without refuge).

Two missions were passed off to me by the Butlers as they departed. I began to work with Sriyani in the Rooftop Ministry and her other missions to the Sri Lankans. I was able, by a promise of sleeping mats and medicines for the 350 women in shelter, to help her get back into the Sri Lankan Embassy, where she got a room to pray with the ladies again. The other mission, which Jeff Butler brought to my attention, was the need for a support system for the Chinese Home Church. In May, I began having regular dinners with the Chinese Home Church pastor and his wife. Sometime later, I also invited another pastor and wife, whom I had worked with in the past but who were not involved in a church at the time, to join us.

<u>Rooftops/Sri Lankan Ministry</u>

In mid-May, I got to help with a medical mission to the Rooftops, my first joint meeting with Sriyani. A friend of hers, named Dr. Saloman, tried his best to treat those illegal laborers who had no access to healthcare. Most were Buddhists, with a smattering of Muslims. Of course, proselytizing is illegal in Kuwait. Sriyani handed me Dr. Saloman's list of required medications, but some of it required prescriptions. I purchased all the non-prescription items, and then turned to a Kuwaiti National Guard physician to ask how I could obtain the remaining items. He took my list and asked me to have one of my guys drop by the following day. Except for children's amoxicillin, he gave me all I needed – God truly smiled on us in that the Kuwaiti government freely gave what I could not obtain. After preaching and then praying over each lady during the visit, we handed out toiletries. Then, Sriyani took the ladies and children to see Dr. Saloman. After he looked through the packages of medicine I brought him, he said, "This is good medicine." I knew we had done well.

We later met with a group of 22 souls, mostly young Christian converts, but included a Muslim, in Jleeb. They asked me to come out regularly with Sriyani as their pastor. I felt so unworthy of their confidence. However, our next trip was canceled by Pastor Martin of the Philippine Ministry, to my great dismay and without my approval. He had gone straight to Sriyani so that I would be available to attend the Philippine National Day celebration to be awarded a plaque of appreciation for the Embassy Chapel support Linda and I had provided. All that day, I felt the strong sense that I was in the wrong place and not in obedience. Sadly, we never made it back to that group of Christians together.

Later, Sriyani and I took a load of toiletries and medicines to the Sri Lankan Embassy. She and I then parted ways to visit our families back in our home countries and agreed to reconvene on the first of August. However, she took a second trip back to her country, so we did not work together again until September. In the interim, I took more toiletries, medications, and 100 mattresses to the Sri Lankan Embassy in her name to keep the door open. We had met twice more in the rooftop area, preaching, providing toiletries, and supplying airfare for four persons (a Bangladeshi and 3 Sri Lankans) to return to their countries during the general amnesty. I then gathered a car full of clothes awaiting our next visit to this group.

Return of Pastor Randall and My Son, Jonathan

In early July, these two, dear people came and served at the Philippine Embassy, the Embassy Chapel, and the Chinese Home Church while I was again a chauffeur and support person. I was really happy to watch my son play and sing at those services. Although much too short of a visit, the time spent with Jonathan and Pastor Randall was very refreshing to me.

A major effort for much of 2008 seems to have been with the Chinese Church. Shortly after connecting with the pastor and his wife at the AECK, where they occasionally attended, I began to provide monthly support in the form of money and foodstuffs for this small in-home church. I began making weekly visits to talk as they had become isolated from the leadership of the Lighthouse Church in Kuwait. (2018 Comment: I did not fully understand the issues between them, possibly because of pastoral confidentiality, but I heard only one side and completely missed the truth – as such, I have omitted a larger, misguided commentary I had recorded since the late Pastor Jerry had such a powerful ministry that should not be deemed less because of my ignorance.) I did attempt to assist the pastor of the Chinese Church in reconciling with Pastor Jerry of the TLC, but mutual forgiveness was as far as they got.

The AECK Council met to discuss a recipient for our August 5th Friday special offering and eventually approved a monthly gift to the Chinese Church. That support continued until the chapel closed in July of 2009. Throughout late 2008 and into 2009, I preached at the Chinese

Church every second Friday, and continued bringing snacks and groceries each Wednesday as part of my coffee time chats.

Filipina Ministry Re-visited

While my other ministries had grown, this one ebbed. The Lord had told me to go where He opened the door, but not to push on the door if man closed it. I had not forgotten the debacle of the canceled meeting with the Sri Lankans. However, I began meeting and preaching at the Philippine refuge again after my son and Pastor Randall departed. In the past, Pastor Martin had always had me prepare a sermon, and I loved speaking to the ladies. However, the opportunity would often be taken away after I had prepared to speak, so I had to stop and reassess the situation. I had just been turned away at the Philippine Embassy gate one Friday morning because the entire meeting had been canceled earlier in the week and Pastor Martin had forgotten to notify me. I found that I was so irritated that morning that I could not worship well during my own service at AECK. Also, the Sri Lankan ministry needed help that no one else was providing. The Philippine Embassy now had many organizations supporting them. While I continued to send toiletries to the Filipinas through Linda Wallace, I decided to cut back my effort and focus on the other two groups so as to devote Friday mornings, which had been used for the Filipinas over the past 13 months, to prayer.

Sri Lankan Ministry Expanded

Our helping the women caught up in human trafficking turned into an evangelistic effort. After the summer of 2008, Sriyani Premadosa returned and invited me to meet her at the Sri Lankan Embassy for a meeting with the warden of the women's refuge there. I vividly remember standing in front of the Embassy compound and telling Sriyani about sensing a dark, hostile presence in that place. This had rarely happened in my life. The last time I had felt this type of presence was when my young family spent the night in Nazareth back in 1993, and Melissa had felt it as well. Luckily, we only suffered a flat tire while we slept poorly that night. In response, Sriyani informed me that it was our job to pierce that darkness we felt and let some light in. We prayed together, then marched into the reception area to meet the warden.

I was not prepared for the misery that awaited me as we followed the warden, an embassy official charged with caring for a large and ever-transitioning group of women housed in the basement of the complex. She took us to the sleeping area for the 350 women, who were crowding around the three of us and trying to understand why some white male in a suit and tie was walking amongst them. The warden said the women slept on the concrete floors using whatever clothes they escaped with as bedding and that more sleeping mats were needed to improve the health of the ladies.

Next, we visited the latrine area. Besides the stench when we entered that room, the first thing that struck me was the broken pipe spewing water across the floor. There was almost no water pressure in the plumbing to run toilets, wash clothes, or shower. There was one large room lined with 12 toilet stalls across two walls. Only two were functional. There was a smaller side room, which may have been a shower room at one time as I spied overhead piping that dripped water, but there were no showerheads. Additionally, there were three small basins, maybe three inches deep, inset into a third wall for which I could see no utility. The warden said the ladies tried to wash their clothes there as best they could. While I set my face to maintain an external appearance of calm, I was horrified with their situation and near tears when I learned that the latrine had been in this condition for almost two years. I learned that the building's Kuwaiti owner refused to repair it and the Embassy had no budget to make improvements.

Next, we toured the kitchen area, pot scrubbing area, and pantry with two refrigerators. The kitchen was a small room with a stove containing one large burner; the floor tiles were uneven and broken. The floors and the soot-stained walls showed evidence of past meals.

Sitting in the scrubbing area were a few large pots used to boil whatever meals were prepared. Likewise, the floor of this area was broken with much standing water. I recalled the four types of foot fungus creams on the Embassy's medication list as I saw this space and thought of all that water sitting in the latrine area.

In the small pantry, the warden explained that the meals were primarily vegetables and rice. They normally had tea and fruit for breakfast. When I asked about meat or fish in their diets, she replied, "Never fish, but, if we had a freezer, we could buy frozen chickens from time to time." Yikes! Almost as an afterthought, I asked if there was any food item that would really be appreciated by the ladies. The warden said milk powder, so the women could have milk tea as they were accustomed to back in Sri Lanka, would definitely brighten their lives. I thought this a simple but effective way to communicate love to a neglected group of people whose language I could not speak.

Honestly, I felt a deep burning anger over the situation of these ladies who had simply left their home country to try to provide an income for their families back home. My brain told me that I couldn't fix this, but my heart said I had to do something. I promised Sriyani to do what I could and return the following week with a plan. Sriyani and I stopped for prayer after leaving the compound, and with a twinkle in her eye, she stated that she was confident the condition of these women would soon improve.

The logistical and operational parts of my mind that years of military experience had refined to a high level had already kicked into overdrive with the enormity of the tasks required to help those desperate people. How could I accomplish any of this? Clearly, the latrine repair and sleeping pad provision had top priority. I sought assistance from the Church council and contacted two pastors I considered good friends to ask for their prayers and any support they might provide. Besides funds from the chapel (AECK) to purchase a freezer for this effort, I also gained assistance of truly great value in another form. The music leader approached me after our meeting and suggested I call her Kuwaiti husband, who had been in the business of remodeling bathrooms and kitchens. When I called, he was most gracious. He offered to let me use his best plumber, Mr. Ahmed, as project lead, and to sell me any supplies necessary at a big discount. I arranged to make another walk-through of the refuge with Ahmed later in the week so I could get an estimate of cost. Then, I concentrated on getting sleeping mats, a chest-type freezer, and milk powder.

So, with support from two U.S. churches, the very able Mr. Ahmed, some greatly discounted fine Italian tile and fixtures, and my own personal budget, we launched into a three-project effort as funds became available. Within a month, Ahmed and his two-man crew had finished the latrine project, which fixed the broken water pipe and all 12 toilets and additionally gave the ladies six functional showerheads and three deep basins to use for washing clothes. I noticed two months after this project that the demand for foot fungus creams had been cut in half – amazing!

The second project, about six weeks later, repaired the kitchen area with smooth tile walls and floors so it could be properly cleaned. The third and final project provided for a special pot-cleaning area, with a smooth floor surface for easy cleaning and a filtered drinking water station. This last project concluded in mid-December of 2008. I owe a debt of gratitude to my two pastor friends (Randall Hosea and Jeff Butler) for their prayers, funding, and advice. We always had just enough money to do each project, and I kept Randall and Jeff aware of what we accomplished with each project. I learned six months later from the Sri Lankan Embassy staff that the Kuwaiti owner had agreed to maintain all of the improvements we had constructed.

Two weeks after the final project, a group from the AECK returned with our annual Christmas bags of toiletries, candy, and new sweaters. The Sri Lankan ladies kept trying to thank all of us for the remodeling of their refuge, but the others were unaware of what had been accomplished in the name of their church.

<u>An Unexpected Invitation</u>

It had been my original intent to support Sriyani's efforts at trying to gain approval to meet and pray with more of her people when she visited weekly. Sriyani informed me just after Christmas that the Ambassador wished to see the two of us to thank us. Frankly, I assumed he wanted to show his appreciation for the three projects to improve the refuge. But, no, those projects never came up during my visit. The Ambassador addressed me at the beginning of the meeting by saying, "Randy, I know you love our people. I know this because you gave every man and woman in refuge here a brand-new sweater still in the cellophane!" (There were 20 men at that time living in a hallway separate from the refuge.) I was surprised and amused by this comment since we had done the same last year. However, my surprise deepened when the Ambassador said, "We only have fifteen Christians in the refuge, but, starting next week, I am going to allow you to hold a Christian service in our Embassy on Fridays at 1:30 p.m." Hallelujah! In order to accomplish this, it would require me having to leave my AECK service 15 minutes early each Friday, but there was only one answer to give the Ambassador – a grateful, "YES, we will be here!" *(Again, I had a front row seat for something I saw as a miracle.)

We had never asked to hold a service within the compound, although that was our goal. I looked to Sriyani, who was elated. On the way out of the Embassy that day, she informed me that His Excellency had specifically said I would hold the service. Sriyani offered her translation services. Knowing she was a great evangelist in her own right who should be leading these services since it was her vision for many years, I quickly accepted.

<u>Sri Lankan Refuge Services</u>
From the start, we never had fewer than 46 souls at our services crammed into the small reception area on the workers' side of the Embassy, and we reached over 85 several times. Sriyani credits our having cared for the physical needs of the people as the reason so many

came out in a show of appreciation. She always knew that more of the women would turn out for a service if ever the opportunity was given, but this exceeded her expectations. Provided with ideas based on a prompting by the Holy Spirit, I came on January 9th in a suit and tie and armed with a small wooden cross and enough oranges for every woman and man in the refuge. The oranges were turned over to the warden before we started so they would not be seen as enticements to the service but as our gifts to all.

There were over 60 at the first service and Sriyani was a pleasure to work with. I noticed that my one sentence pauses for her translation often seemed to cause her to say six sentences. As I mentioned before, she was an able evangelist in her own right. Now she had a pulpit, and we saw 12 souls come to own Jesus as Savior and Lord that first day. We were both thrilled. She stopped me after the service to tell me that I would never know how much it meant for these women, who had been treated as dirt, to have an American man come speak to them in a suit and tie. Without knowing it, I had raised their self-worth through such a small act. It became part of my armor for going to do battle on a spiritual plane from that day forward.

The January 16th service had 86 souls in the reception area at start time. The response was around 40 women coming forward for the prayer of salvation. That day, I was called "Father" by some of the Catholic ladies and, whether I was preaching or delivering medications during the week, the name stuck. I felt a bit of a pretender by allowing it, but Sriyani advised that I accept this title since they meant it as an honor. I also began worrying about discipleship for the new converts, since several ladies had been repatriated since our first meeting, but the Holy Spirit said to me, "That is not your job, just stay on mission."

Things worked well into mid-March, but Sriyani's friend at the Embassy said a third level foreign affairs person was complaining to the Ambassador about our conversions of Buddhists and Muslims. However, this did not impede us as we had no control over who came, no access to the refuge to invite people to attend, and the Warden was clearly a friend to us.

On the mornings of March 27th and April 3rd, the Embassy Chapel was temporarily meeting off-site so repairs to the multi-purpose hall on the compound could be made. On March 27th, I met Sharon Orleans Lawrence, who would later become my wife. She had been brought to church by our piano player, and she noticed that I had to excuse myself from the AECK service early to attend the Sri Lankan service. But, more about her later.

A Demon Came to Call

Our Sri Lankan service on March 27th was a watershed event in two very important respects, as you will see. As I called everyone into the room for the opening prayer, two women helped a third woman they carried between them to a place in the back. That third woman was mumbling and looked to be on drugs. She was given a seat on a bench with the two women standing next to her to keep her from falling off. Sriyani, having taken the previous week off, had taken her customary place beside me, and another friend from the chapel was standing at the back to observe this ministry for the first time.

There were only 46 women this day as I preached from 2 Corinthians 5:15-6:2. During the sermon, whenever I said the name "Jesus" or "Jesus Christ," the mumbling woman called out in crisp, American English, "Stop saying that name!" She also spoke Sinhala during Sriyani's translation to the same effect. In my mind, I thought, "We have a bilingual demon possessing this poor woman. Please Lord, tell me what to do! I know what Jesus and Paul had said, so just order me, please!" I had no real training in this. Yet, silence was all I heard in response.

Being military in my thinking, I just kept pressing on while waiting for the Lord to speak to me. As the service culminated, four ladies came forward to accept Jesus as Lord and Savior. While I started to lead them in prayer, the mumbling-stumbler ran unaided past me to the back of the room, screaming for me to, "Stop saying that name!" I immediately lost my translator, as Sriyani had followed her to the back, repeatedly reciting, "By the blood of Jesus," while touching her shoulder. The two women who had led her in were standing on either side of her, neither knowing what to do nor understanding her English statements.

Since I could not go on with the prayer without my translator, I followed them to the back of the room as well and asked the demon-possessed woman if I could pray for her. She went silent, so I placed my palm on her forehead, and, before I could utter a word, she collapsed on the floor. While mildly shocked, I knew all eyes were on me, so I asked the ladies to carry her to the side and for Sriyani to rejoin me and the four seekers of salvation.

It was not long into our resumed prayer when I heard the mumbler again crying out even louder, "Stop saying that name!" At this point, she was distracting me, and during Sriyani's translations I was begging the Lord for guidance. I then remembered that I was to stay on mission, so maybe casting out demons was not my calling. When I had had enough of the yelling, I closed my eyes, turned my face downward, threw out my left hand in her direction, and shouted, "Silence!" I immediately heard a crash. Looking over, I saw her prostrate body in a heap on the floor. I turned back to the praying as if nothing strange had happened, completed the service by taking time to pray over each seeker, and offered to stay for prayer with others.

When I dismissed the service, and saw the two women drag the comatose form out of the room, I felt like a complete failure for not casting out the demon directly. I also went away thinking that one or more of those four women was so important to the Lord that the Holy Spirit showed His power like I had never before seen.

When I asked the accompanying Chapel friend what he had seen, he quickly, and in an embarrassed way, said he had no idea what had happened. Sriyani, however, had seen and heard exactly what I had experienced. There had been a spiritual combat that I couldn't see with a real woman being held in bondage by an evil force. *(Again, I had a front row seat for something I just could not fathom.)

Chapter 2: Grief and a Call to Ministry

The following is an excerpt from an email string that I sent to Pastor Jeff Butler the day after this confrontation:

Jeff,

The discussion is helpful. This is completely new for me. The things I have been pondering are these:

1. Why did I feel no fear? Afterward, I realized that I had always thought I would be scared of such an event. I know I was focused on the seekers of salvation, but it seems the Holy Spirit made this event a minor sideshow. Sriyani was focusing on the demon-possessed rather than the ladies. She later said I was completely right to silence the demon and keep going. I told her it was not me doing the silencing.

2. While everything I did in this regard was while praying to my Lord, I felt so unprepared, yet Jesus kept control on the situation despite my weakness. Is there a lesson I can use again without making it arrogance or superstition? I never felt strong or in control and believe there was a battle in the spiritual realm right in front of me that I could not see or even sense.

3. There is a soul in desperate need of help in that body, but when I asked the Lord if I should order the demon out in His name, I got no peace to proceed so I did not try. I am concerned for that soul and feel I should fast in this regard. I am no exorcist and have no promise of success should I try.

I feel that I should not go hunting a confrontation but be better prepared and if the Lord brings us together again, maybe I will have freedom to be a part of liberating this poor woman,

Any thoughts on this? Randy

April 3rd proved to be our last service. We again had over 50 souls in the service, and I was accompanied by Sharon Orleans Lawrence from the Chapel, who, being very nicely dressed, actually waded into the crowd of women that day, hugging them and praying for them, and they reacted with delight towards her. Sriyani and I saw another eight come forward to pray for salvation.

Demon-less

About two weeks after the demon came to call, I arrived at the Sri Lankan Embassy with two large boxes of medications, as previously scheduled. As I began to exit via the reception area, I suddenly met the same young woman who had been dragged through that same reception area on March 27th. She meekly approached me and in broken English pleaded, "Father, please pray for me!" as she fell to her knees in front of me, wrapped her arms around my knees, and sobbed. I placed my hand on her head and sensed no evil presence. I then thanked God for His power and removal of the evil spirit. Without a translator, I led her in a prayer for salvation, hoping her little English would be enough for her to understand. I never saw her again after that day, but I will be looking to meet her again in the not too distant future. *(Again, I had a front row seat for a miracle.)

Destined to Fail, or Mission Completed?

I have missed those services at the Sri Lankan Embassy and wondered what I might have done differently. I found comfort in thinking we were put there "for such a time as this" (words from Esther 4:14 when Queen Esther's uncle spoke to the Queen before she took her life in her hands by interrupting the King of Persia). Also, I knew our evangelism among Buddhists could not be helpful to the Ambassador, so continuance was doomed by God's success those last three months. It seemed the demon-possessed woman coming into her right mind had been the last straw, since the reports by the other women left little room for alternative theories – a fear of the name Jesus had fallen on the occupants and staff of that place.

61

Despite that setback, I continued to visit the Sri Lankan Embassy to bring medications. A few weeks after our services ended, the Warden saw me as I was dropping off supplies and asked me to visit their sick room in the refuge. I saw and prayed over three ladies while there, but again, the Warden knew "Father Randy" would help in other ways. One lady had suffered two broken legs from her escape attempt through a third story window. She hadn't been paid for over eight months and had suffered some physical abuse when she complained to the family for whom she worked. Another had a cold. The third was a 21-year old woman dying of late-stage lung cancer, but she did not know what was wrong with her. No official, neither medical nor embassy staff, had told her the diagnosis or prognosis.

I cannot describe the emotions that struck me at that moment. I arranged with the Warden to return in two hours with funds to cover flights back to Sri Lanka the following day for the lung cancer patient and the woman on crutches. The Embassy staff had the tickets ready when I arrived, and those two poor souls left Kuwait as arranged. I did not have a translator to communicate with the Tamil-speaking cancer victim, but I could make sure she died with her family rather than in this prison of another kind.

I must admit, in retrospect, that God seemed to be giving me a timeout from the Sri Lankan services to get to know Sharon better, because she, unbeknownst to me, was destined to play a large role in what was about to unfold in my next spiritual mission – pastoring.

Chapter 3. A New Mate and a New Ministry

"The Lord God said, 'It is not good for the man to be alone. I will make a helper suitable for him.'" Genesis 2:18 (NIV)

The Sharon Paradox

Sharon Orleans Lawrence – there is no simple or short way to describe this woman who suddenly breezed into my existence that Friday morning in March 2009. She was highly skilled at most things creative: writing, singing, dancing, drawing, painting, metal-sculpting, design, and speaking – but to the Nth degree. Except for speaking and some limited singing and writing, this left brain of mine had none of those skills. She was like my polar opposite on the skills chart. Oh, and she took her artistry from the atelier into the kitchen! This writer of six cookbooks could do magic when given time, a few basic ingredients, and someone to wash up the pots and pans

Heroic scale 48" x 48" masterwork titled "Talk to Me" (Oil on canvas) by Sharon Orleans Lawrence, 2007.

(she could dirty every pot in a kitchen to prepare a single meal!).

When she first met me, she thought I was still a married man by the way I acted and the ill-fitting clothes I wore. She came early that Friday morning while I was setting up for the service in a villa that the Embassy

Chapel was borrowing for two weeks. We always had coffee and tea available, so she drank tea and chatted with me about the church as I went about my business. I learned that she had come to Kuwait in August of 2008 to start a fine arts program at the American University of Kuwait but could not find a church or a ride to church until that particular day.

My first impression was that she was highly intelligent. Now, dear reader, it is okay to think that an odd thing on which to focus. Back when I was in the 8th grade, a teacher asked my classmates and me to list the qualities we would like in a future spouse in priority order. I was laughed at by the other boys when I read that *intelligence* was first on my list. Their lists, to a boy, started with *beauty*. So, in my world, this mention of intelligence was high praise. However, I also noticed she had beautiful green eyes and a full head of auburn hair.

She saw that I left early to go to the Sri Lankan Embassy to preach and later asked to accompany me to that service, so I agreed to the April 3rd service if she accompanied me to a late lunch. At that lunch, I learned that she had been initially raised by her grandmother and then her mom and Coast Guard stepfather. She had been married more than once, and was tired of men going to church so they could date her. She had decided that if she ever married again, the man would need to be someone already busy serving Jesus.

So, while I was trying to decide if I should date again, my traditional Baptist upbringing told me I could not date her because she had been divorced. I remembered from the Sermon on the Mount when Jesus said that any man who marries a divorced woman commits adultery (Matthew 5:32b). "Ah well," I thought, "and she seemed worth getting to know more than any woman I had met these past three years." Then one night as I was left with my loneliness and wondering if God would bring someone special my way, the Voice told me He already had and said, "Do not call anything impure that God has made clean." – I remembered that verse from Acts 10:15b when Peter was being called to minister to Gentiles. What in the world was I to do?

This became a several-round argument with the Holy Spirit. Eventually, He told me, "Do or don't do. Either way, it will be okay.

You'll just miss a blessing." He had me again. But how was I going to explain this to my Baptist brothers? I proposed in early June, and she quickly agreed with great happiness. She turned out to be exactly what I was missing.

End of the American Embassy Chapel of Kuwait
(AECK)

In early June of 2009, I received a letter from the U.S. Ambassador that both the Protestant and Catholic Chapels would close by the end of August 2009. Since we would be in the middle of summer vacations, the Council agreed to find other accommodations by the end of July. I replied to the Ambassador accordingly, thanked her for the use of the facility, and said I would continue to pray for her success. Pastor Dave Peacock arranged for our group to start meeting in a time slot at a facility in Jabriya that the TLC was renting. Since there was already a music ministry in place and no role for our leaders, the AECK simply disbanded.

I bought half of the communion dishes and Bibles that were on hand before departing for vacation. Having been involved in the establishment of the AECK in 2002 and returned in 2007 to see that the Chapel had left its initial role, it seemed somehow proper to now be there to see it fall apart. Even so, it was a bit saddening.

I spent some of July visiting Melissa's mother and sisters to inform them in person that I was about to remarry. I was relieved to get their blessing, and they inquired much about Sharon. While I was at the family farm in southern Missouri, my ability to stay in contact by text, as Sharon and I had been doing, ended. She had a panic attack thinking that I had possibly changed my mind. Well, I called her one evening and was quickly and thoroughly reminded that a bride needed constant contact with her groom in the days before a wedding. During that conversation, I also learned that she and her daughter Rachel had found a wedding dress.

I realized that life as a single guy had allowed me to forget some important husbandly lessons that I once knew so well.

When I arrived in Morehead City, North Carolina, things moved very fast getting the license, venue, and wedding party in place. I hit it off very well with Sharon's family. Her dad, Bobby Lawrence, was a career Coast Guardsman and retired as a Master Chief. When I introduced myself and addressed him as "Sir," he reminded me that he had been a proud enlisted man that did not tolerate being called "Sir" because he worked for a living. I had been an officer, so it wasn't right; he insisted, "Just call me Bobby." I responded that my mama back in the Ozarks might slap me if I did not refer to my future father-in-law as "Sir." Then, I declared for the entire room that, from that day forth, I would call Mr. Robert Lawrence "Sir Bobby!" We fell into instant like, and he was Sir Bobby until his passing in November 2012.

Sharon Orleans Lawrence and I wed at Ft. Macon Beach on August 4, 2009, standing beside her daughter Shea, the bridesmaid.

On August 4, 2009, we were wed by Pastor Jerry Linebarger of the Open Door Baptist Church on the beautiful beach at Fort Macon Park. Everything went so smoothly. Sharon's eldest daughter, Shea Garrison, was the bridesmaid, and two of my sons, Joshua and Jonathan, drove up from Riverview, Florida, for the event. However, my vacation time was much more limited than Sharon's vacation period, so we had two days at a hotel on the beach before I returned to Kuwait. I left her with my promise of a proper honeymoon at Christmas.

Beginning of the International Christian Fellowship of Kuwait
(ICFK)

Four days after I returned to Kuwait, that same familiar voice woke me up before dawn, saying, "It's time to start the Church." I didn't need to ask because I remembered the "Lead My People" directive from 2006. Now, Sharon and I had shared no discussion previously about starting a church, so I had to begin this conversation with her. When I called her that day, she did not sound thrilled about it and reminded me that in ancient Israel the young men were given a year off from soldiering when they got married. I should consider the same. Before Sharon returned to Kuwait during the second week of September, I had met with about ten people to share the instructions given to me and see if they were willing to join me. Six agreed right away, and the others joined within a few weeks. I also enrolled with International Seminary of Plymouth, Florida—a ministry associated with Assemblies of God and a supporter of military chaplains and overseas missionaries. Protestant denominations were almost non-existent in Kuwait since there were so few authorized places for Christians to gather. My thinking was that I would need to know more about other denominations to pastor a non-denominational church, and, as the Army was short on chaplains, I could be flexible in case I did not get the message clearly. The blunt instrument had swung into action again.

Within a year, I completed a Certificate in Practical Theology that also came with an ordination as a reverend as I continued to pastor a small, but growing flock. What I came away from seminary work with was an appreciation that my Baptist background and the Assemblies of God teachings agreed on over 95% of all I studied. I set my mind to focus on teaching Bible only and avoiding points of tradition as best I could. I chose not to major on the minor points and to choose good people who shared a salvation experience to fill positions of responsibility. In the end, I learned from them other traditions, and they learned from me. When I had to leave the church in late 2015, we were working in one accord on many fronts, which included outreach and service to the impoverished and lost. I also studied some lessons on listening to the Holy Spirit that I later found relevant.

Anyway, back to our story.

Upon Sharon's return to Kuwait, we organized a first meeting with potential congregants for the new church to pray for direction. We both became disturbed when some of the group showed up with organizing documents, like bylaws, and took over the discussion so there was no prayer. Sharon wisely advised me not to surrender the vision given me by the Holy Spirit to others who were not given that same vision. It seems that I should have called a halt and started over, but this blunt instrument was still swinging.

I contacted the IRS for disenrollment of the American Embassy Chapel of Kuwait as a charity and to begin formation of the International Christian Fellowship of Kuwait as a charity. My "friends" in the IRS made it simple: by way of a single letter, a set of minutes, keeping the same EIN, and a name change, they accomplished both actions quickly.

I considered myself to be a tentmaking minister, after the Apostle Paul's example, as I took no payment from the church but instead held a vocation to cover my needs as I served Christ. This later became a point that drew new members and also protected me from concerns that my popularity might cost me my livelihood. This latter problem has occurred too often to godly servants that I have known.

Growth
(late 2009-2012)

We began in the home of one of the group and continued there for several months, picking up a trickle of people as the days went by. By early 2011, we had moved into a small hall built on top of an apartment building, constructed by a Kuwaiti just for our use. We shared time in this space with Dr. Ehab Saieed's small Arab congregation to keep our rent lower and to give him access to space that few Kuwaitis would allow an Egyptian Christian to rent.

I shared preaching duties with another ordained minister whom I had once worked with at the AECK. The Holy Spirit always gave me plenty of material to speak on by the usual means of illuminated Scripture or a catch in the Spirit as I carried on my daily Bible readings and prayer. Sharon had been our first praise leader, but some rudeness by a man, old enough to know better, caused her to want to quit. He insisted there was "only one good style of worship music, and Sharon wasn't doing it." I tried to shield her, but to no avail. She stepped down (with all her talents) in early 2010.

I recalled that Charles Haddon Spurgeon called his music ministry "The War Department" because of tussles over music style. I eventually had to speak to this issue. I grew up with Southern Gospel quartet music. Yet no one was singing that in Kuwait, nor did I think that style was required. The Praise Leader would pick the music with an occasional non-binding suggestion from me. If anyone did not like the music style, I let them know they were welcome to see me with their repertoire, and I would arrange a day for them to lead the singing. Until the day I left, not one person took me up on my offer. When the issue came up in Council, I merely voiced support for our Praise Leader. I also learned to appreciate different music styles – as long as the lyrics were in line with Christ's teachings, I became a fan. I learned that there has been some great music produced over the past few decades that seem to mostly be Psalms or other verses from the Bible set in song. It seems fitting to sing Scripture back to God – hard to improve on, as well.

Before long, the Arab congregation was made unwelcome as Arab speakers around the apartment were offended by hearing praises to Jesus in their native language. So, we all left and began using a hotel, which allowed us to grow more quickly. However, it also brought us issues concerning our growing group of children and youth with whom we were being blessed. I am a big fan of kids, so I was serious about solving this problem. We rented a large hall weekly, as well as two smaller rooms for the kids, which was a very expensive solution. Despite that, we were making our budget. Due to the nature of our expatriate congregation, we would fit in one medium-sized hall in the summers as 70% of our flock would take vacation as one.

In the area of finances, I initially tried to create a budget without knowing expenses or income. From the outset, I took responsibility to account for and keep the congregation aware of how monies were spent and what our needs were. I became immediately aware that we had few attendees that were committed to tithing. I also created an "Outreach" line in the budget that would go primarily toward local ministry. From the start, I would present the annual church budget and lead a question and answer session on that budget before it was put to a vote of approval. Additionally, I would audit the books, kept by the treasurer, and file our records with the IRS. However, I did my utmost never to be responsible for cash. The changes in banking laws after 9/11 made it impossible for our church to have an account in Kuwait, and the one we had in the U.S. provided limited assistance. We were forced to use cash, a safety deposit box at a local bank, and a two-person accounting system in an attempt to prevent fraud. That system worked sufficiently for the first forty-two months and then failed in traumatic fashion, but more on that later.

Sharon and Joshua Williams

Sharon and I decided to gather our two sides of the family, along with our parents, at a beach house in North Carolina in August of 2010 during the week of our first anniversary. It was stressful in many ways, but a great thing happened for one of my boys that week as Sharon asked Josh to consider coming to Kuwait to finish his bachelor's degree at AUK. By then, Josh was already low on options as Blockbuster Video, where he worked, began closing stores. He immediately applied, arrived in Kuwait in September of 2010, and began his studies with the understanding that he had two years and one summer semester to complete his degree. I required that he do volunteer work at the church and my other charity, and he would seek work as he could. With Sharon on staff, his tuition was very affordable. Sharon was tough on Josh, as was I, but she was tougher. She gave him a second chance that I thought, at the time, was purely crazy.

In May of 2012, Josh graduated "with great honors" and having obtained a BA in English Literature. He also had a pending job in South Korea and a record of achievements which included representing his university at a conference of the Sigma Tau Delta International English Honor Society in New Orleans as well as volunteer work with AUK, the church, and the Association of the U.S. Army – Kuwait Chapter. He spent his summers at my parents' farm with my instructions to watch my father because that is how I learned to be a man. To me, his crowning achievement was the article he wrote in the AUK newspaper in the spring of 2012 thanking Sharon for her support and guiding hand in his obtaining a college degree. He matured in many areas during his time with Sharon. She had proved good for my family, even though the two other sons might not have agreed at that time.

PTSD

On the work front, I faced a new challenge that called for help from Sharon and my team of guys, as well as cooperation from an airlines executive, a Kuwaiti doctor, and a retired Army colonel (named Val) at my company headquarters. On the advice of a retired Marine Gunnery Sergeant I knew; I hired a former Marine NCO who had good explosive ordnance disposal (EOD) skills to train Kuwaitis. What I did not know was that he was being treated for PTSD. As a covered disability, he did not have to disclose the condition to employers, so he ended up on my team in Kuwait. About half-way through his contract, his condition revealed itself in a terrible way. He admitted that he had quit taking his medications before he left the U.S., thinking that he was healed of the problem. He did not even bring the medications with him to Kuwait. Then, he suddenly got worse. I contacted the U.S. Navy Captain in charge of the small U.S. military hospitals in Kuwait only to be informed that the U.S. military could do nothing for him since he had not retired and only had eight years of service. The Captain was very helpful in saying that the VA back in the U.S., was his only support system.

I had to figure out how to put someone on an international flight who could no longer communicate, beyond occasional grunts, and had a paranoia that made him hold on to anything he could grip to prevent anyone from moving him. His eyes told the story of fear and a complete lack of understanding about what was happening to him. As a Ranger student, I had been instilled with the tenet that we never leave a fallen comrade behind. While this man and I had never served together, my entire team considered him a comrade who had to be helped. That was another time of intense prayer for guidance.

As I sought help for him, I learned that the Kuwaiti Hospital for psychological patients did not recognize PTSD as a mental condition at that time. The Egyptian doctors there wanted to keep him under observation for two weeks. Meanwhile, company lawyers were advising my bosses to reject my suggestions of contacting the VA, as well as talking to any medical expert on the issue, due to privacy laws. The company for which I worked had transformed into something very different than the one I had joined, as retired military officers no longer ran it. It seemed that leaving him in limbo was the only course of action left to me. That was unacceptable to every fiber in my being.

I awoke one morning with a plan of action that came to me in response to prayers. I will not give many of the details of the rest of this story, leaving that to this young man, since it is his to tell one day. I realized that I would have to violate some rules, and maybe even some laws; nevertheless, I kept members of the U.S. Embassy staff, the airline executive, and air marshals via the airline employees apprised of my plan. I also shared everything with the VA analyst in Colorado who had been working the case of our ill comrade.

My senior translator and I had to use every ounce of persuasion at our disposal to pull off the feat of getting our plan to work. We took charge of the patient, and members of my team took turns watching over him until we took him to the airport. A policeman on my team volunteered to escort him back to the States. I bought the tickets – a downside of the plan was bearing most of the costs of flying both individuals.

We used a wheelchair to bring our now sedated comrade to the airport. The entire team assembled to see him off. His escort carried additional sedatives to be given to the medically trained airline attendant. He was also able to get word to the air marshal about his ward.

As the plane began its descent into Washington, DC, the sedatives were weakening, so the grunts started disturbing other passengers. The escort wisely spoke to the attendants about disembarking in Washington rather than continuing on to Denver. The escort deposited our comrade at a hospital with ties to the VA, and they took control of him. Val was able to get me the doctor's contact information, so I called and gave him my observations as well as contact information for the VA Analyst in Colorado. Thankfully, my bosses did not want to know the details of this repatriation.

From time to time, I exchange emails with our comrade beset with PTSD. His last email informed me that he was back with his wife and two sons and had a job helping other PTSD cases near a Marine base. Sharon was proud to be a part of that effort, as were my employees, so I keep them informed as I can. Maybe "for such a time as this" we were there when that great need arose. It may not have been a miracle, but it felt like one to me, and it helped a helpless man who had fallen through the cracks of normal safety nets.

Tensions Arise

Sharon excelled at organizing musical programs to accompany my sermons on special holidays. So, as I alternated leadership at the Easter and Christmas programs with my fellow pastor, I would rely on Sharon to assist me when my turn came around. At the Christmas service of 2011, her work with the various singers and choir was outstanding. Yet, as we met to put the audiovisual together and run through the order with everyone on the morning of the Christmas program, things looked to be set for disaster. Our guy on the computer could not find the lyrics for the songs or music for Sharon's solo. He had to be pressured into stepping away from the computer with mere minutes before start time so Joshua could try to get us back on track. He did so with one minute to spare. One lady came late for the service preparation and got upset when Sharon had no time to speak to her about her part. This led to the other pastor's wife complaining harshly to Sharon as she and Joshua were in the throes of solving the computer issues. However, Sharon was a consummate professional and did not let the stress show as the service began.

It was probably our best Christmas service while at the hotel. Sharon ended the musical portion by singing a solo of Casting Crown's "I Heard the Bells on Christmas Day." It was easy to preach after her song. She brought out both the strong sense of strife on earth and the peace that God was trying to give us that first Christmas morning. This sort of resembled what I was seeing in our church as the service was being prepared. Thankfully, none of the congregation had seemed to notice the strife that had occurred that morning.

The following week, as the service concluded, Sharon stepped up to give a final prayer and the announcements. After dismissal, three members of the leadership team attacked her verbally, and I had to step in. They had misunderstood one of her announcements as a criticism and began yelling and belittling her efforts in the excellent Christmas program that we had witnessed the previous week. It all struck me as childish jealousy, so I called a halt to the mess and told them we would meet as a team later and not to impact the congregation with this negativity. On the way out, I checked with one of the congregants who must have heard it all, but he said he heard nothing. That seemed impossible given the decibel level of the rancor, but he was clearly being honest with me.

The next week, we took toiletries, candy, and sweaters as Christmas presents to all of the refugees at the Sri Lankan Embassy. As we assembled to depart for the refuge, one of our ladies stated that we should not touch the Sri Lankans for fear of disease. I clearly failed to stop that virus (of another kind) from spreading to the other volunteers. As we passed out the gifts, we again told each recipient that Jesus loved her, but there were no hugs other than what Sharon provided. I then led a Christmas service for them and ended with offering to pray for them. We seemed to have a misunderstanding in translation as the entire group of about 35 ladies all stepped forward as one and knelt to be prayed over. Only Sharon joined me, as the other leaders and few congregants held back. Some even drew back, as if repulsed. I hid my anger. However, my wife waded into the group, praying, touching and hugging them. I was so very proud of her.

So many missed the healing of human touch that night – this had never happened previously. From that point on, I instructed any volunteers that if they could not touch the refugees then they were not to come along with me.

I met with my fellow pastor after returning from a week away in Europe with Sharon and spoke to him about the petty jealousies that seemed to have sprung up. The discussion seemed to end well. But when the entire leadership assembled at my apartment in early January, that meeting ended in open hostility toward Sharon.

Sharon and I in the Netherlands in January 2012 after we viewed much art at the Rijksmuseum and the Van Gogh Museum.

After they departed, Sharon stated that she could not attend the church any more. So, I told her that I could not pastor there if she was not at my side. By the time the next service rolled around, she decided to attend with me; while she would not volunteer for anything, she did continue to serve in any capacity I asked of her.

My fellow pastor seemed to put less into his preparations for preaching at that point, but I am not sure why. One sermon contained two poems but not one verse of Scripture. Members of two families let me know that they would avoid attending if they knew he was preaching. Then, Sharon added a new offense. She began doodling in her sketch book while seated in the front row if the sermon meandered. The pastor told me that bothered him. When I mentioned it to Sharon, she refused to consider another course of action. I promised to tell him to spend more time in preparation and less time on the golf course should it come up again.

Two Betrayals

Let me begin by saying that anyone who betrays me has not done a greatly heinous deed, but to betray a congregation that belongs to Jesus Christ is quite serious. I think the cost of such action will prove to be huge. In the early fall of 2012, my partner preacher and three other council members abruptly left the church without a clear explanation of what the problem was. It somehow had to do with Sharon being obedient to "Church Leadership." They wanted her to sign a paper submitting to the "Church Leadership." Sharon's doodling in her sketch book, when she was frustrated with a poorly prepared sermon, was seen as a sign of disrespect.

As her husband and a church leader myself, I took umbrage at the time, since my wife held no position in the church. I told them she was respectful to me and asked them to show me a scripture where a document like that was used anywhere in the Bible. The bottom line was they did not return, so my preaching requirements doubled. I was unfamiliar with a pastor just walking away when there was no effort to drive him out. It seemed a betrayal to the flock. However, the replacement council members turned out to be really good for our future.

A Thin Man Appeared

We set a meeting with a conflict resolution counselor to discuss our impasse. The resolution counselor, who was also a recent new member of our small congregation, agreed to meet with the three former church leaders, Sharon and myself; however, the night before the meeting, a strange thing occurred. After mulling over the issues I thought might be raised, I fell into a deep sleep from which I awoke in a sudden panic. When I opened my eyes, I saw a man standing at the foot of the bed, which caused me to bolt upright, waking Sharon. In a flash, the man ran to my side of the bed, and, as he came beside me, he disappeared. He seemed to have been slightly tall and very thin. Oddly, I felt a deep peace where panic had been. Sharon asked me what happened. When I told her, she matter-of-factly said, "It's just an angel. Go back to sleep and quit worrying about tomorrow." *Easy for her to say!* Then I thought, "Why is she so calm about this, and why do I feel so calm?" In the serenity of the moment, I drifted quickly back to sleep.

The next day's meeting was strange as the leading complainant had trouble putting his thoughts together, coming across to Sharon and the mediator as being nearly lunatic. The mediator asked the complainant's side for a second meeting, to which they agreed, but they never followed through. I have never quite understood this entire episode with my former friends and co-leaders, nor the appearance of the Thin Man. However, it is my hope that some readers may make sense of why God sent this messenger. It had left me scratching my head, yet Sharon seemed to grasp it even though she had never seen the fellow. *(Again I had a front row seat for something I saw as a miracle.)

At this point, church health improved as the numbers of congregants were growing and our income had increased greatly. We had amassed a large surplus so the new council members were discussing the rental of a villa so we could do multiple services, provide for our kids better, and have a kitchen for community meals. All this would be at less than what we were paying for the hotel spaces. I remember looking around during one service, seeing that we had representatives of seventeen different countries in the congregation, and realizing that this was just a small picture of what heaven will be like. We needed to provide a better facility for God's people.

Our Christmas event at the Sri Lankan Embassy in 2012 was so much better than the previous year. There were more people to put the gift bags together, and no one shrunk back when the opportunity to pray over these women occurred. I felt, at the time, that we were suddenly stronger as a church than ever before. The Holy Spirit had added to us by subtracting from us.

However, a terrible shoe was about to drop in early 2013. It seems that the two council members responsible for the safekeeping of our funds were more loyal to self and friends than to God and His church body. All those surplus funds disappeared, as did half of the offering records. The remaining offering records had been falsified to show collection for two weeks on one paper, rather than the single document per week that we had practiced for the entire year. For those sheets to be correct, there could never have been any loose cash collected—only checks. Two of the remaining falsified forms had my signature on the bottom, along with the treasurer's signature, and I knew I had not signed such a form. Also, we had always received loose cash, but those two forms read otherwise. It then became easy to track down other signatories on the remaining forms, and the resulting responses by those signatories were denial of having signed an altered form. Like myself, the others had signed a single week collection document.

I now understood why the financial records had not been turned over to me in a timely manner despite my constant requests. When I did get them, I had barely a week to file with the IRS. I was glad that the Elders had taken control of the cash immediately after their ordination in late March.

Both men responsible for the missing funds refused to answer questions or speak to our investigating Elders when contacted. They had already left the church to join with the leaders who had just previously departed. My heart broke as these were both men I had trusted. What bothered me more was that we lost a few very devoted Christians because of friendships or lack of full understanding of what had occurred. I cannot blame this last group for walking out. They had done nothing wrong, but it did hurt to see them go. I did not feel I could speak openly with any of them until an investigation was completed. I could only speak to the Council. However, the two perpetrators did not restrain themselves similarly.

Resolution

My one saving grace during this chapter of the church will sound like the start of a religious joke. With our growth and my need to shed some responsibility so as to focus on preaching and guiding, I had interviewed and installed our first three Elders – an Anglican, a Lutheran, and an independent Baptist married to a Brethren Church lady. With a mostly Southern Baptist as pastor – can you see the punchline? Additionally, I referred to Sharon as a Papal-costal when introducing her to others in the church, which always drew puzzling looks and a laugh. Sharon grew up in traditions similar to mine but loved the freer worship of Full Gospel and found her artist skills more respected among Catholics. She told me that mainstream Protestant congregations tend to look at highly skilled artists with distrust. It's a sad commentary that I saw play out myself. I think the touch of perfectionist that makes great artists so great also plays a role in this but highly creative people ought to feel welcome among the rest of us.

I began referring to the Elders as my three wise men (Alan, Jeff, and Bill) when speaking to Sharon. By the way, their jobs were Financial Investor, Bank Examiner, and Conflict Resolution Specialist – only the Holy Spirit could have known beforehand what was coming and what our church needed in its leadership. I am just not that clairvoyant. Their wives, Sandy, Laura, and Susannah, were as intelligent and talented as their husbands, so the ICFK was in good hands should anything happen to me. Furthermore, Simon and Alicia (not their real names) took over the music ministry in a very spiritual and professional way.

When the aforementioned loss of funds and altered documents were discovered by our Assistant Treasurer, I went to the three Elders. They asked me to keep my hand on the tiller of the ship as they sorted the matter out. Our lead Elder in this matter, who was also a bank examiner, declared it the clearest case of fraud he had seen in his many years of service to the banking industry. I loved those men as brothers; we were one in Christ. They also told me that they all felt a villa was what our church needed and that we needed to pray accordingly, despite this loss of funds. What faith like this can be found in most men?

By late May, I did have to get involved when the two obstructionists threatened my Elders with a lawsuit the following week if the Elders persisted in accusing them of theft or if I informed the church families of the loss as I had planned. I told the Elders that they had gone as far as humanly possible. My morning Bible reading that Tuesday in preparation for preaching was from Ephesians 5:1-14, as I was working my way through that book. The illuminated passages were: "But among you there must not be even a hint of … any kind of impurity, or of greed because these are improper for God's Holy People… No … greedy person… has an inheritance in the Kingdom of Christ… Have nothing to do with the fruitless deeds of darkness, but rather expose them. For it is shameful to mention what the disobedient do in secret." When I learned later that day of the threatened lawsuit and that some of my Elders showed real concern, I already had the answer – expose those deeds of darkness. I informed the Elders that they could wrap up their investigation because God was now fighting for them. I proceeded as if the obstructionists would carry out their threat of lawsuit as I wanted to minimize within the church the bad news that would surely hit the Kuwaiti press.

The boss of one of those two perpetrators was a dear friend of mine and Sharon's, so I decided not to have him blindsided. However, that evening, before I had a chance to call him, I just happened to meet him at a U.S. Embassy function. When I mentioned needing to speak privately with him, he immediately invited me to his house. This friend was not a church-going type, but we had worked together a lot and he always displayed good sense. When I arrived at his apartment, I got straight to the point. "Your employee has information on the loss of church funds but will not share his information with the Elders investigating the matter," I explained. "Then, today he threatened a lawsuit in Kuwaiti courts if my Elders kept inquiring or if I explained the matter to the church, indicating that he was involved in the loss." My friend asked if his employee had taken the money. I answered that I had no way of knowing but that I did know he had to have been involved in handing over the large surplus we had had, even if he did not keep any himself. I explained that I needed my friend to do nothing but simply be aware of what the issue was for when the court case broke in the papers. He said, "Okay."

Early Friday morning, I got a scathing text from a former church member, who had nothing to do with this issue, accusing me of taking church business outside the church by talking to my friend. Hmmm! I guess a court case must not be considered by this fellow to be "outside the church." I did not respond to the text but knew my friend must have said something. Two hours later, I gathered the heads of the families of our church to explain to them the loss. I then allowed the Elders to explain the new three-person checks and balances system with quarterly audits we established to prevent further loss. The news was difficult for the people to hear, but they all stayed with the church. Hallelujah.

Attendance and income began to grow again, and we suddenly realized that we had been being bled by about 50% of weekly offerings by the former financial team. When November rolled around, we had the funds to consider looking for a villa. A few of us kicked in additional monetary gifts, and we did indeed make a contract on a villa to begin occupancy by December 20, 2013.

The Holy Spirit was so right. I could not have made it to this point without Sharon by my side—and occasionally taking a starring role. His idea to install Elders, as I read from Paul in his letters to Timothy and Titus, was truly a key piece to the stability we now enjoyed. The Three Wise Men and I met to pray each month at one of our homes and only to talk business as time allowed. This one routine action led to a closely coordinated approach to all facets of our efforts.

Chapter 3: A New Mate and a New Ministry

<u>The Villa</u>

Thanks to my stellar Elders and their wives, we arranged during the first week of December to be able to actually move into the villa by December 20th. This vision for a villa had come true quicker than any of us had thought possible when we had met in June to pray for this. Many thanks to Bill and Susannah Schuillenburg for agreeing to move into the upper rooms. That saved us money and provided for responsible leadership on site. Then Pastor Ehab paid some toward our rent so his congregation could use the facility. Of course, the ever-active Alan Dempster organized our move in so efficiently we actually began to worship in the villa on the 20th—with an agreement to hold our grand opening ceremony on January 17th. That way, all our people could be back from vacation, and our decorating team would be able to make the main assembly hall ready for use. There was a hall that could seat 120 and another in the basement that could hold 70 persons. There was a huge kitchen and a large entry area that we used for meals and Sunday school as necessary. There were two smaller Sunday school rooms, a nursery, a pastor's study, and a couple of storage rooms. Also, Bill and Susannah kept a room upstairs for any visiting pastors. Sandy Dempster helped me as the new secretary and in numerous other ways, including keeping Alan's prodigious mind for trying new things in some kind of pace I could keep up with.

At the Grand Opening, the hall was packed. As I stood to welcome everyone, the Voice whispered to me, "This was the reason you were sent to Kuwait. **Your mission is accomplished."** Sadly, that was the last time I heard the Holy Spirit speak to me in words. Things went well for the church like never before. We had good, solid, Christian men and women show up, ready to work to make their church a success in Kuwait. Another highlight was in May when we held our first baptism for seven souls.

By March 2014, our congregation, as well as the Arab Congregation, had increased significantly. We were now able to have a more logical budget system, and we remained very open on how monies were used. As we pledged a tithe to outreach, our giving increased. We initiated routine reports to the church on the outreach efforts, often having the reports presented to the congregation by those in charge of each effort. This included some work in Iraq, other areas of the Middle East, and Africa. Furthermore, we always put more into local work where our people could be discipled by more experienced church members in how to do ministry. These small steps also led to increased giving for outreach.

With the Three Wise Men overseeing the villa, our finances, children's church, administrative issues, and a web site, I was freed to concentrate on preaching, discipling, and local ministry. This was not to say that I did not have knowledge of those areas, because our monthly business meetings kept me informed. I also participated in quarterly counts of money as well as the annual audit and IRS filings.

Simon took the lead in our Easter service and arranged for a large rough-hewn cross towered in the center of our meeting space with all congregants facing that cross. The Holy Spirit held court with us that day as each attached their name to that cross to show their sins were forgiven and Christ Jesus was their Lord.

In May of 2014, Bill arranged for a portable pool in our courtyard, and we baptized seven folks, most of whom were deeply involved in various ministries. I met with each candidate to assure myself that Christ was indeed their Savior and Lord. It was during that time that I was confronted by the issue of cultural Christianity as opposed to spiritual (biblical) Christianity. I met with a Lebanese man whose wife encouraged him to be baptized with their daughter. He had only attended our services twice and claimed to have been a Christian his entire life, as had many generations of his forbears. However, he had never had a time when he asked Jesus to forgive him of his sins, nor had he committed his life to Christ. I then had a chance to explain Biblical salvation and lead him in a prayer for that salvation.

Let me fast forward a moment to tell you that, a year later, we had a great set-up for our ministries. Plus, we hosted the Kuwait Ladies Bible Society at no charge, expanded our classes and gatherings, and added a teen ministry. There were often three home Bible studies available during the week, led by some of our leaders. We increased support to the poor (that involved our members), and I got to hold a Christmas service at the Sri Lankan Embassy again. This time, there were many hands to put the gifts together. Also, at that service, there were many hands to distribute those gifts, many voices to say "Merry Christmas, Jesu' Swansa obada oderei (Jesus loves you)," and many willing to pray and give hugs as opportunity presented itself.

When I sat down in December 2014 to see where the church stood financially, I found we were paid two months ahead on rent and in surplus held approximately the same amount that we had determined as the minimum loss to fraud in 2013 (about $22,000) – now tell me that God doesn't have a great sense of humor and gets the last laugh! *(And, again, I had a front row seat for God doing something awesome.)

It's Happening Again

As 2014 wound down, Sharon's health became poor, and she really had a difficult time in London and Edinburgh where we met Christopher and Rachel Titus for Christmas and New Year's Day. After we returned to Kuwait, her scan on January 11th revealed a tumor on her pancreas. I immediately made arrangements for her to return to the U.S. for a second opinion and decisions on treatment. At UNC-Chapel Hill Hospital, Sharon met with her daughter, Shea, and her mother, Jean Lawrence, where the diagnosis was confirmed as stage-4 pancreatic cancer. Sharon and Rachel decided on Cancer Treatment Centers of America-Goodyear in Arizona as her place of treatment, so I flew to meet them there. Rachel volunteered to act as primary caregiver so I could return to my job in order to keep the excellent medical insurance intact.

While I gave Rachel my hard-won lessons as a caregiver, I knew that no words could prepare her for what was to come. I had previously told Sharon how God had told me what would happen with Melissa, so she kept asking me about herself, but all I got was silence from the Holy

Spirit. Sharon got really sick at CTCA, and both she and Rachel were in despair. Then Rachel found one of the best pancreatic specialists was near her home in Los Angeles, so we moved Sharon there in March. When I returned to Kuwait, Sharon spoke of her worst night at CTCA when she saw several very thin angels in fine Italian pin-striped suits hovering around her bed. She said she drew comfort from their presence. This sounded very familiar to me, except for the Italian suits.

The year was a roller coaster ride for all of us, particularly Sharon and Rachel. I made six trips to the U.S. to be with them. In Kuwait, we installed two new elders: Simon (an ordained minister of Salvation Army background), who, with his talented wife, Alicia, led our praise and worship efforts; and John Michael "Mike" Miller (Church of Christ), who, with his very intelligent wife, Christine, led one of the weekly Bible studies in their home. Those two replaced Bill and Jeff as they returned to Canada and the U.S. respectively. My previous comment on opening lines to a religious joke would still apply with us.

On my job front, the new corporate team seemed unwilling to give me the lead to negotiate, and the new Kuwaiti team I worked with was very inflexible. As it turned out, I would be leaving Kuwait in December. I regret my guys losing their jobs, but I was so thankful that Pastor Simon agreed to step into my role at ICFK. I advised him not to feel constrained to run things as I had but to let the Holy Spirit guide his leadership. He was already an outstanding preacher and worship leader, and my new Elders agreed to support him. I attended the Christmas program as my last service and enjoyed an eight-piece musical ensemble, including a cello and violin – who would have ever thought? This group had talent to spare! Maybe they were really set to grow but needed a new leader at the top. (Comment: As I write this in mid-2018, I still follow the ministries of the ICFK and celebrate their successes. May God continue to protect this church and its ministries.)

For my part, I must admit that my mind was not good for many months. I shut down a business, handed over a church, and relinquished another charity for which I was president to return to the U.S. with no job and a sick wife.

<u>Death of My Partner – Again</u>

Poor Rachel bore the brunt of the caregiver's burden during 2015, but she and Sharon grew closer than ever. After March of 2015, Sharon's scans revealed steady shrinkage of tumors and cancer markers. I tried to assume primary caregiver duties upon my return but found that Sharon felt much more secure with Rachel, so I was often a second caregiver.

There were so many pills that Sharon had to take throughout each day for digestion, blood pressure, neuropathy, and more. Sharon always had her own mind about things, and, once her mind was set, dynamite could not move her off that stand. Well, taking all of her blood pressure medicine was one of those things that she just refused to do. In mid-March 2016, she had a scan showing neither a tumor on the pancreas or liver nor that cloudy mass of tumor cells in the nerve network beside the pancreas. We were ecstatic.

Then, the doctor said that her blood pressure was so out of control that he feared a stroke at any moment and said he would seek a better blood pressure medication and adjust his chemo away from what he had been using. Things just seemed to fall apart after that.

The pain block she had received at UNC in January 2015 began failing by May of 2016, and her pain became unbearable by degrees. On June 29th, I took Sharon to see her doctor about the pain, and he recommended Sharon go to an emergency room that was much better equipped to help her—but Sharon refused. The doctor tried several medications until she finally quit hurting and gave us meds to see her through the next day, when we were to return so he could see how she was doing.

That evening, she snored quite roughly and was mostly incoherent, but she seemed not to be in pain. The next morning, I arose early to work out at the gym upstairs and found her snoring lightly. After my almost two-hour workout, I returned to check on her and found her not breathing, without heartbeat, and with a grayish froth coming from her mouth to the pillow. I immediately recognized this as a reaction to a poison, took the fentanyl patch off her skin, and rubbed the area with a dry cloth. Then I moved her onto the floor and began CPR as I dialed 911. The operator was quite competent, and within five minutes of the call there were Sherman Oaks Fire & Rescue EMTs in my apartment. Just before they knocked, Sharon had taken her first shallow breath.

My military training allowed me to rapid-fire on what I had observed and done, so they administered Narcane and oxygen. While I sat on the couch observing those great professionals at work, I notified both daughters that their mom was unresponsive – maybe not the best phrasing. Rachel and Chris were on the east coast performing at comedy venues, and Shea worked in Washington, DC.

The EMTs eventually found her pulse, weak but strengthening, so they transported her to the nearest hospital. When I got to the ER, I met two of the five EMTs who had worked on her and was soon joined by Rachel's friend, Amber Thompson, who proved a great help that day. When the doctor came in, Sharon was still unconscious but stable, and I heard that her heart had stopped for two minutes according to his tests and that if I had been much later in returning she probably would not have made it. That thought put it all in a different perspective. I knew I had little time to help her, but I thanked God we got another day.

Rachel arrived later that day. We had exchanged multiple texts, and I heard from both girls that "unresponsive" is not a good thing to send. Ah well, I blamed it on my military training. Sharon had indeed fit that description. We spent several days at Sherman Oaks Hospital before being released.

After hearing she had died for a short period, Sharon went about changing everything she could about our bedroom. She painted a new, cheery canvas to hang over the bed, and we changed sides of the bed so she was not in the same place where she had died for those two minutes. Out went the old bedspread and linens, and in came new things.

It still took two more months before the blood pressure was under control and a new pain block finally worked. There was no chemo during most of this period, and the cancer returned at a ferocious rate. By September, Sharon was pretty much done with chemo and opted to attend three weeks of cleansing her body at the Optimal Health Institute in Lemon Grove, California. Rachel was with her the first two weeks, and I took Rachel's place for the last week, which was early October. This was just after I returned from Daegu, South Korea, for my son Joshua Williams' wedding to a lovely young lady named Pilsun Jung. Sharon did have a short spell of feeling better from this cleansing.

I left Los Angeles, with Sharon's encouragement, to help at my parent's farm in November and to officiate my youngest son Jonathan's wedding to Kiersta Castagno near Tampa, Florida, on December 10, 2016. Shea had joined Rachel to be with Sharon during my time away. On the evening before I returned, Shea phoned to inform me that Sharon was not acting right. As I was landing in Los Angeles, I received a text that Sharon was in Sherman Oaks Hospital, unable to think or speak clearly.

The Night Watch

She was in poor condition and unable to use a call button should she need help, so I assumed the duty of staying with her through the nights and much of the days. I listened for her moans of discomfort and other sounds that told me she was in need of help. While it was not at all restful, I could not see myself doing otherwise. We then transferred her from Sherman Oaks to a UCLA hospital.

What we learned during a month-long hospital stay at UCLA–Santa Monica was that the cancer had clogged bile ducts, causing sepsis, as her liver began to die. I assumed the night watch again as Sharon had no ability to use a call button and was only sometimes coherent. Her family gathered in her hospital room to be with her for Christmas, her favorite holiday – one that she always tried to make special for each member of her family. She missed opening her presents and finishing wrapping ones she intended to give, but she did enjoy the grandchildren and children around her hospital bed. We even had a nice Christmas dinner from Izzy's Deli in her room.

She was released in early January, and her primary doctor recommended hospice at that point. I don't wish to describe the gruesomeness of the hospital stay or that final month of her life in our small apartment. I did find pleasure in her kids coming back again. She liked having them around her. While it was a bit crowded, and sometimes others were disturbed by my night watch duties, it still felt right.

In mid-January, Joshua brought his wife, Pilsun, to meet the famous Sharon he had described to her. Sharon was hardly able to communicate, but we could see the appreciation in her eyes. We also had a visit from Jonathan and Kiersta in those final two weeks of her life. As the dying liver released ammonia into her body, her ability to communicate verbally ceased. I have to say this seemed a much crueler form of cancer than colon cancer, as that great communicator could only form small words and disjointed syllables.

Rachel got to hear her final words, "Best…Friend" during those last days. I knew Sharon realized her time was short, so I spoke into her ear a promise to stay in Los Angeles for a year to see that Rachel would be okay. Again, I saw appreciation in her eyes, but she was not able to respond otherwise. During the early afternoon of February 5th, I saw a change come over Sharon and told her kids that it would not be long. That evening, the hospice nurse told Rachel that her mother was hanging on due to concerns for her. So, Rachel spoke to her honestly that she would not be okay, but she would get through somehow. A few hours later, I heard Sharon's final breath in the early hours of February 6, 2017.

As a family, we held the funeral service for Sharon Orleans Lawrence Williams in her beloved Morehead City, North Carolina, according to her wishes as we knew them. Being an artist, she usually chose the path less taken, and, although some thought her service irreverent or having very repetitious songs (Sharon's favorites), I knew it was what she wanted. We held a second memorial for her many friends and admirers back in Los Angeles a week later at Bel Air Church, and it was simply a celebration of Sharon's life among many admirers.

My life, it seems, had just gone from 90 mph to zero in just over a year. I knew not to make any big decisions, such as taking a job back in Kuwait. My focus was in seeking the Lord for guidance in my new small life as to what He wanted me to do after my year in Los Angeles concluded. With only silence, I committed to volunteering and helping others where I could. I made many friends in the area and enjoyed my time with other believers at Bel Air Church. I cannot say enough good things about Pastor Kim Dorr-Tilley and the deacons at Bel Air Church in LA, as well as Yoshi Kitabiyashi, Sharon's masseuse and friend, as the battle exceeded two years.

Unfinished oil on canvas (23 of the planned 36 layers of oil) by Sharon Orleans Lawrence, begun in Kuwait summer of 2013 and last touched in early 2016 by the artist. Titled, "I Am Not Finished Speaking Yet" by her husband in keeping with her style of naming after her death.

Once again, I tended to mourn in private so others did not see my tears. I do think that part of my heart was still numb from my previous loss. Readers of my first draft of this book were surprised at my humanity and the depth of feeling they discovered since I was so stoic in front of them. Since I became an adult, I have always joked that I only have two feelings and no one can hurt both of them simultaneously. That is far from the truth. It is my hope that my family understands that I do hurt from this episode, as well as the first loss. I just wonder if I will have less heart to give to my loved ones in the future.

Another Note to Caregivers

I have seen during the loss of both wives and Sir Bobby that, as death approaches, their hearing becomes ultra-sensitive, and the mind is generally working well. They are easily bothered by noise, and visitors may think it is okay to talk about the apparently comatose person as if they cannot hear what is going on around them. **You must act as sheriff in these instances to stop the conversation or send them out**. You may find the dying one becoming agitated. For example, in 2012 when I returned to Morehead City to be with Sharon during Sir Bobby's last days, I walked in, grabbed his left big toe (knowing his right side was paralyzed by stroke), and said, "Sir Bobby! Randy is here!" He had been lying completely still for some time with his eyes toward the ceiling, yet he responded as a military man might: by saluting me with his left hand. The entire group around the bed gasped, and some said that if they had known he was listening they would not have been saying the things they had. **It is okay to hurt some feelings when trying to make those final hours less stressful for your patient.** I will remember that salute for the rest of my days.

Keys to Grief Recovery

Continue with all of those caregiver survival techniques, but **get out of your house to socialize. Specifically, find ways to help those less fortunate than yourself, read, and go to movies and interesting places**. Oddly, one of the best tools that helped me after that first loss, and also helped me in the next chapter of life, was to **memorize long passages of scripture** while taking my Doberman for a walk. I managed to memorize all 111 verses of the Sermon on the Mount (Matthew chapters 5-7) in less than two weeks. I noted with pleasure that my Doberman never criticized when I messed up my recitation. He thought I was talking lovingly to him. Later, as a pastor, those passages proved quite valuable. But that was not remotely in my thoughts in 2005.

During my week at the Optimal Health Institute, they put on a talent night for the patients to display their skills. After Sharon sang some Patsy Cline and Martina McBride songs, I got to follow a Buddhist 'Om and gong' session with The Sermon on the Mount. It was surprising that such an educated group had little familiarity with the greatest sermon ever preached – Jesus, God the Son, spoke to us of things from the very throne room of His Father.

Most importantly, mark your calendar a year out from when you bury your loved one and, as much as humanly possible, make no big decisions during that year. Your mind needs to heal, and you need to get somewhat comfortable in your new situation before striking out in a direction you may quickly regret.

Specifically, **do not try to find a new mate in this period**. Some of the most miserable people I have met in my life were those who remarried about six months after such a loss. Additionally, when you do think you are recovered enough to consider remarriage, do not fall into the trap of fooling yourself that that other person has the same personality, goals, opinions, likes, and dislikes of your former mate. It never happens. You must learn the new potential mate to the degree that you can accept that one as he or she is and love that person above all other humans. If you cannot, then do not yoke yourself to that person. This advice (putting a new man in her life above her offspring) is probably harder for women with children to consider. But, I beg you to consider that God designed marriage to be a man and woman leaving their parents to become one – a team. Discuss these things openly with a potential new partner so the two of you can do the best you can.

Advice for When the Holy Spirit Speaks in Unexpected Ways

If you are unsure of what you are hearing, pray about it and do as Gideon did in Judges 6:36-40. It likely won't be a fleece, but give the

Spirit an opportunity to respond in a miraculous way to confirm His intentions. Then, trust Him! He certainly came through on my job in the Kuwait challenge.

The Holy Spirit is a gentleman in that He won't force you to do anything. However, He wants the best for you, which is something you likely cannot see. Once I gave up arguing and doubting, our relationship became very efficient. I truly miss that close relationship when I would hear Him speak. I know He is still there, and likely to surprise me again with a new task – I certainly hope so.

The best advice I received from a pastor as I pursued ordination was: *If you don't have to preach, then don't preach. But if you feel constrained to preach, you better get after it.*

This jewel came from Sharon: *The Holy Spirit gave you the vision and the orders. Why are you giving away that vision to others who clearly have not bought into the vision?* In other words, when the Holy Spirit gives you a task, you own it. You can bring others into the mission and create roles or listen to their thoughts, but, if you allow them to drag you off course, it is your responsibility to get things back on course.

If you call a meeting to pray for vision or anything else and someone brings an organizational document or some other item to discuss rather than pray, stop the process and get to praying. You can always set another meeting for the other item, but do not cut prayer short in the beginning, middle, or end of a sacred mission from the Holy Spirit. This was my first and greatest mistake when trying to start the church. I will never allow that to happen again. It took us three years and a lot of pain to recover.

I always found evangelism easier and more fulfilling than pastoring. However, if you disciple a church well, they can do exceedingly more in evangelism and everything else than you could ever do by yourself. Pastoring well is just plain hard work – and don't expect appreciation. Let the Holy Spirit be your cheerleader and mentor – listen to Him and the mate He has given you. If you have great Elders as I did, give ear to their thoughts as well as the thoughts of their spouses – they are a team, so trust them as a team.

Sit with anyone you might consider for church leadership. Tell them your conversion story, then listen to theirs and what they have done for Christ since that conversion. You will learn tons about that person. If they are married, meet the couple along with your spouse and have a conversation. Sharon and I together always walked away with a very good idea of the grounding and potential of that couple. The Holy Spirit was speaking to us separately as those conversations progressed. This process served us very well after late 2012.

Satan is no gentleman. He knows your greatest weakness better than you do and will attack it, so figure it out and place guards on your life. No one suddenly slips up; it is a steady erosion of boundaries. Engage your spouse and the Holy Spirit to protect your ministry. My wife was my greatest weakness and suffered many attacks from the congregation and at her place of work (I am certain Satan was leading that), so I spent much time distracted from the main goals until I got this under control.

When you feel weak in the face of strong opposition, pray to Christ for strength, wisdom, and peace. He gave those to me when I asked. He also gave unexpected outcomes that seemed to suit His plans rather than mine. I just had to realign my plans with His plans.

Keep following your last orders from the Holy Spirit until He reveals a new mission or revised instructions.

Finally, and this is no joke, there were times of turmoil when I found the most spiritually effective thing for me to do was to take a short nap after prayer. My hard-charging nature rebelled at this bit of advice when it was passed to me by a wise friend. Yet, it proved amazingly true as I often awoke with both ideas and energy to tackle that next obstacle.

<u>Guardian Angels?</u>

I have mentioned two occasions during my military career that, when I was desperate, God seemed to intervene to make me a success in the face of pending disaster. In one case, I believe an angel presented himself as a senior officer in an instant when I called out to God for help.

In retrospect, it is also possible that helping me to attain senior rank provided me with additional income upon retirement so I might more readily serve Him without taking a salary from the church. There have been other times when some event diverted my path, and I either avoided danger entirely or walked through the danger without harm. Some call it coincidence, but it seems to me that God had plans for me that were yet incomplete. One day, my mission will be done, and that angel may be the one who takes me home.

I had not thought much about angels helping us mortals, although I certainly believed I had received such help. I was in awe since it was so unexpected. Recently, I read the story of Abraham's servant going to find a wife for young Isaac. Abraham told the servant that an angel would go with him to make his mission successful. Each time the servant asked for God's help or a sign, it occurred as he asked. Yet, the Bible does not record that servant ever seeing the angel. I would never consider testing a relationship with this heavenly being, but it has been a comfort to know that there is one nearby to intercede at God's command when I cannot solve one of life's dilemmas.

Maybe that is how that Noah's Ark globe started playing on June 1, 2006. I had a sense of peace in that moment. Like all of the other times, a sense of calm replaced the stress I had been feeling. I will share one more of these events in the next section.

Chapter 4. Another New Phase of Life

"Trust in the LORD with all your heart
And do not lean on your own understanding.
In all your ways acknowledge Him,
And He will make your paths straight."
Proverbs 3:5-6 (NASB)

Rancher Randy – A Work in Progress?

After spending the promised year trying to be available to Rachel, I became aware that my aging parents were not keeping up with their farm. These two had provided me with near-Norman Rockwell raising in rural Missouri. Since I had no new missions from the Holy Spirit and did not want to involve myself in something that could be hard to pull out of when the call came, I returned to my roots. I now find myself learning the intricacies of cattle ranching while I await that next call to ministry. This provides my parents with a sense of safety, and I don't have to worry about my 80-year-old mother keeping up the farm now that I am with them daily.

Together, we are shoring up all of the deferred maintenance items and making the farm work more efficiently. We have restored a 40-acre field, where floods a couple of years ago had ripped out fences and created water gaps, to useable pastureland.

Mom now has time to take care of Dad and his health issues, and she can leave the farm for doctor visits without worry of loss in her absence. She is aware that I have told the Lord that I will go anywhere He sends me. I just need Him to let me know clearly as He previously did. Until those orders come, I will be the church where I am and work to be the best rancher I can be. I am already the best stock dog that Mom has – a joke between us, since her dogs are not much help!

In my spare time, I am reading *Veterinary Guide for Farmers*. I also own four heifers. The first of those heifers, I just happened to be in the right place at the right time to save her life. One particular morning, I woke up at 4:45 a.m. and had a cup of coffee. Then I decided to go to the field to study three stumps I needed to remove that day. There was a full moon and no other man-made lights, so I could see my targets fairly well; however, I could not see the black Angus cows around me in the lot we called the "maternity ward." I was surprised to suddenly see a newborn calf come toward me on wobbly legs, but, when I reached out to touch her head, she recoiled in fear. However, I was more surprised to see the calf shoved back to me by a large black mass looming behind her. Newborn calves fear humans, and momma cows almost always protect their calves from all animals. So, I was a bit shocked, but I understood the cow was trying to tell me something was wrong. After inspecting the calf and then the cow by moonlight, I saw the momma cow had no milk bag formed, so she could not feed her baby. This was a cry for help, and the clock was already ticking. The calf needed colostrum and whole milk very soon. So, I woke my mother, and she happened to have one bag of colostrum in the freezer. We fed the calf by bottle for five days until she was actually able to drink from the cow. That is how I obtained my first cow and some really cool photos of bottle-feeding her.

I still have my quiet times with my Lord, but I also spend more time praying and thanking Him during the course of my days. Maybe the slower pace here makes that communication easier. Oh, and I also have time to read and write.

Not Forgotten

Recently, I came to believe that God wants me to be a success at ranching. A sudden storm with heavy winds, rain, and lightning took down five trees, knocked out over a dozen treetops, burned a round bale of hay, and ripped a large barn door off our main equipment building.

This scared the fourteen heifers who were waiting out the weather nearby.

The largest of the fallen trees, an enormous, spreading oak, had mangled a stretch of fence, snapping wires, when its roots became vertical and the trunk horizontal. This occurred in the lot we use as our maternity ward for expectant cows. Removing the tree and restoring the fence fell to me as a top priority since it was only six weeks until calving season arrived. While I am fairly adept at handling a chainsaw, this monster tree was held up by large branches, and the trunk was suspended in the air by its large root wad. I decided to work inward to the trunk, removing the many branches as I went. I eventually had to walk along the trunk to cut two large limbs that were vertical. Much prayer preceded each attempt, and both fell exactly where I prayed they would. Then, I started on the uppermost part of the trunk. As I cut about halfway through the trunk, it sagged, pinching my saw blade. I attempted to relieve the pressure by hammering a wedge into the cut above the bar of the saw, but it just would not open a large enough gap. Instead of getting frustrated, I remembered thanking God for keeping me safe through those two dangerous cuts and said, "I guess you thought I needed a break to go get the old chainsaw out." After only taking a couple of steps toward the vehicle I was using, I heard a loud crunch and a small thud behind me. When I turned, I saw the wedge was no longer in its place (small thud), and the saw was hanging loosely in the cut, which was now open. As I pulled the saw out, I asked out loud, "How does several tons of oak tree that was pressing down toward the earth suddenly reverse course so I get my saw back? Oh, and I guess that You *don't* think I need that break!" I just chuckled and went back to work, wondering why I felt so peaceful.

Final Word of Advice

Do not approach this kind of challenge (being a caregiver) as a burden, or you will develop a poor attitude toward the loved ones you came to care for. I keep the same routine of Scripture reading, prayer, exercise, diet, and volunteerism to keep me sane and useful. Sometimes, I even write a sermon that may eventually be delivered when I am once again constrained to preach.

Be encouraged. Many have faced the ash heap that was once their dreams only to live a good and enjoyable life beyond that moment. When I sat down to write my story, I recalled my vision of the ash heap, so it naturally fit into the title. On August 22, 2018, as I read scripture from I Samuel chapter 2, I discovered that Hannah, the eventual mother of Samuel, the prophet, high priest, and last judge of Israel, also saw her life of barrenness as an ash heap that her rival, Peninnah, tormented her with often. In her desperation, Hannah prayed to God for a son, whom she promised to devote to the Lord's service. When a son was born, she kept her promise and composed a song of praise that was recorded for posterity's sake. Verse 8 of the chapter records, "He raises the poor from the dust and lifts the needy from the ash heap; he seats them with princes and has them inherit a throne of honor (NIV)." The Lord heard Hannah's plea and ended her barrenness with a son she named Samuel (meaning *God heard*). The Lord further rewarded her with five other children after she delivered Samuel to the Tabernacle. So, know that God hears your mournful cries and stands ready to bless you. Don't give up! It is likely that His answer will catch you by surprise and bring joy again into your life from an unexpected place. He did so with my life, and I believe He has done likewise in every generation.

The End (For Now)

"I know both how to be abased, and I know how to abound:
every where and in all things I am instructed both to be full and to
be hungry, both to abound and to suffer need.
I can do all things through Christ which strengtheneth me."
Philippians 4:12-13 (KJV, 1769)

"...and, lo, I [Christ] am with you alway,
even unto the end of the world. Amen."
Matthew 28:20b (KJV, 1769)

ABOUT THE AUTHOR

Randy was born in St. Louis, Missouri, and raised in rural areas southwest of that city. After graduating from the business school at the University of Missouri-St. Louis, and completing R.O.T.C. at Washington University, he joined the U.S. Army as a second lieutenant in May 1981. He married Melissa Ann Simpson in December of the same year, having just successfully finished Ranger School. They headed to Germany for the first of many assignments. They had three sons, Nathan, Joshua, and Jonathan, and together they traveled widely to four other continents. Randy spent over 11 years in the infantry but transitioned to become a Middle East Foreign Area Officer after completing Arabic training at the Defense Language Institute in Monterey. They then had tours in Jordan, Tampa, Florida, and Kuwait. Randy lost Melissa to colon cancer in October 2005, and retired from the Army a year later. He also completed Masters of Arts degrees in Geography from UNC-Chapel Hill and in Strategic Studies from the U.S. Army War College in Carlisle, Pennsylvania, during his Army service.

Randy was then called into ministry and took a job in Kuwait as a program manager, under a State Department Technical Agreement, to train security forces. He used his available time to follow God's call of leading His people. While in Kuwait, he met and married Sharon Orleans Lawrence, an accomplished artist and educator, in 2009. They started a church together and traveled throughout Europe, visiting the most prestigious art galleries every chance they had. In early 2015, doctors discovered Sharon had pancreatic cancer, and she passed away in Los Angeles in early February 2017. Randy still counts Sharon's children—Shea Garrison, Joshua Bradley and Rachel Bradley Titus—as family.

He considers himself a doer rather than a writer, but friends and colleagues convinced him to share his lessons as a caregiver, a bereaved husband, and a man of God. If his experiences help even a handful of people, he will consider this a worthwhile project.

Randy currently assists his parents in running their cattle ranch in southern Missouri while awaiting a new call to ministry.

Made in the USA
Columbia, SC
10 March 2019